D1179531

THE FORTIFIED HOUSE
IN SCOTLAND

THE FORTIFIED HOUSE
IN SCOTLAND

NIGEL TRANTER

VOLUME FOUR

ABERDEENSHIRE, ANGUS AND
KINCARDINESHIRE

JAMES THIN

1986

THE MERCAT PRESS, EDINBURGH

This is a reprint of the 1962 edition,
to which some new material has been added.

© 1962 Nigel Tranter

ISBN No. 0901824 45 3

Printed by Billing & Sons Limited
Worcester

PREFACE

THE area covered by this fourth volume of the series which is to include all Scotland, comprises only the three counties of Aberdeenshire, Angus, and Kincardineshire; and since the number of buildings described, 104 in all, is similar to that dealt with in each of the previous three volumes, totalling between them 19 counties, some idea of the richness of this area, in fortified houses, may be gained. Aberdeenshire, indeed, is by far the most generously endowed county in all the land, in this respect, both in numbers and in the quality of not a few of the fortalices, which here reach the very peak of Scottish domestic castellated architecture, in structures such as Craigievar, Midmar, Castle Fraser, Fyvie and Drum. The compiling of this volume, therefore, has been a very real joy, long anticipated—but a joy that has been tempered by a grievous list of casualties. Despite the large number here described and drawn—52 in Aberdeenshire alone—the author was unprepared for the large number that have gone, many in comparatively recent times. And saddened by the numbers which undoubtedly *will* go before long, unless the public conscience is awakened, and speedily, to the widespread danger to this irreplaceable and splendid national heritage. Some 250 ancient properties were visited and explored in this great county, since it is desired that *all* fortified houses of the period, in which at least the main features survive, should be included; inevitably the greater proportion of these were bound to be found to be hopelessly ruined, so altered as to be unrecognisable, or swept away by demolition—but to find only 20 per cent remaining was a distinct disappointment.

The same applies all over Scotland, of course. Early in this series the author, perhaps rashly, hazarded a guess that there might be as many as 1,000 of these unique buildings remaining in a fair state of entirety; but now, with four volumes completed and more than half the country covered, it is evident that the total is going to be nearer 600—not because of any miscalculation as to numbers, but owing to the rate of wastage.

It is to be emphasised that it is not only, or even mainly, sheer age and the elements which are responsible; it is human neglect and worse, authorised vandalism. The breaking up of estates, the difficulty of maintaining and staffing country houses, and the decline of the landed gentry—these modern conditions create a state of affairs where it is, all too frequently, apparently nobody's business to guard and spare these ancient fortalices, built to resist armed attack, from the present-day attacks of demolition firms, planners, road-wideners, and 'improvers' generally. Above all from an attitude of mind which is apt to equate age with obsolescence, usefulness with modernity, and progress with sweeping away and 'dinging' down. Unhappily, despite all that has been said and written, this mentality is still strongly entrenched amongst local authorities, which instead of being the guardians of the people's heritage in this respect, are almost its greatest menace. Such authorities more and more become the owners or controllers of so many of our castles and ancient mansions, as cities spread, towns develop and social services reach out into the countryside. Even as this is written, Edinburgh Town Council is threatening to demolish the early 17th century Pilrig House, which it has owned for many years and not used—as, since Volume One was published, it has demolished Niddrie Marischal. Merchiston Castle was only saved after a fight. The Capital, of course, is no worse than other cities in this respect. Surely the possession of these sturdy, characterful buildings, attractive in themselves as well as monuments to our colourful and storied past, is not only one of our most precious inheritances but a vital enhancement of present-day mass-dominated living conditions—and one which the rest of the world does well to envy us.

Here, as before, great fortresses and military strengths are not included; nor are town-houses, which were not normally fortified. Although some of the castles, like Cairnbulg, Broughty and the old tower of Drum, date from as early as the 13th, 14th and 15th centuries, the great majority belong to that tremendously potent and productive period between 1550 and 1650, when the belated Reformation was breaking up the vast Church lands and parcelling them out amongst great numbers of small proprietors, each of whom was required to erect a 'house of fence' thereupon, as a condition of the royal grant—largely with a view to maintaining law and order in an age before police forces. The fact that, by and large, they seem to have had the reverse effect, their strength encouraging their lairds to cock a snook at central authority, while sad from a moralist's point of view, now only adds to their almost uniformly colourful history.

The author, who has made great efforts to ensure that few, if any, houses of the period have been missed out, is largely tilling virgin ground in this respect, there being no country-wide comprehensive list of such structures, the Ancient Monuments Commission's work being a long way from completion. As always, he acknowledges his great debt to that wonderful work of McGibbon and Ross, *The Castellated and Domestic Architecture of Scotland*, long unfortunately out-of-print and now unobtainable save at vast cost. He has had the usual problems over borderline cases, deciding for instance, not to include Birse Castle, Aberdeenshire, which has been built up round a mere fragment of original work, although in identical style; yet including the Place of Tillyfour, where much the same applies, though with considerably more of the original surviving. Where to draw the line with ruins is also sometimes a problem, as when including Forter and Finavon Castles in Angus, and yet rejecting Ballinshoe Castle in the same county, only slightly more ruinous. A general impression of the original appearance has had to be his guide, with at least the main features still evident. This is a work, it is hoped, of general appeal; whereas to the expert a few feet of masonry, or even the shape of grass-grown foundations, may reveal much, to the average viewer these remain but 'rickles o' stanes' and of scant significance.

It is the intention to include in the final volume, probably Volume Six, those buildings which the author has discovered to have been missed out in earlier issues, throughout the whole country.

Scotland, partly out of national character, partly from historical conditions and lack of centralised control, and partly because of the prolonged links with France, produced a flowering of castellated architecture unequalled elsewhere, in vigour and strength tempered with grace. Here is a monument to something vehement, vital and enduring in our nation. Let us cherish it.

The author would take this opportunity of thanking all those who have assisted him in the compilation of this volume. In particular he would acknowledge the help received from Mr Fenton Wyness, Aberdeen; Mr Cuthbert Graham, of *The Aberdeen Press and Journal*; The Librarian and Staff of Aberdeen Public Library; and Mr and Mrs Maurice Simpson of Muchalls Castle.

CONTENTS

[11]

ABERDEENSHIRE

ABERGELDIE CASTLE

This attractive fortalice, famous for its present-day royal connection, stands on the south bank of the Dee six miles west of Ballater and three east of Balmoral. It is a simple oblong tower, with angle-turrets crowning the two northern angles and a semi-circular stair-tower rising at the south-west corner, corbelled out to the square at the top to form a watch-chamber, this being surmounted by a balustraded flat roof and an ogee-roofed belfry. A clock has been added at watch-chamber level, and an unsightly modern dormer-type window inserted nearby. The walls are roughcast and whitewashed, and the gables crowstepped. The

basement is vaulted and the usual arrangement of kitchens there, Hall on first floor, and sleeping accommodation above would prevail. The building has certain similarities to the rather smaller Knock Castle nearby.

Like Knock, Abergeldie was a Gordon stronghold, the lands having been acquired by Sir Alexander Gordon of Midmar, second son of the 1st Earl of Huntly, in the second half of the 15th century. He died in 1504. His grandson James, third of Abergeldie, was slain at the Battle of Pinkie. The 4th laird, his son Alexander, acted as Bailie to his kinsman the Earl of Huntly, for his Deeside properties. *His* fourth son was George Gordon of Knock, who died at the Battle of Glenlivet, when the Catholic Gordons were in revolt against the forces of King James the Sixth, in 1594. It was a grandson therefore, Alexander Gordon of Knock, whose seven sons were slain, whilst digging peats, by the Forbeses—and another grandson, William, of Abergeldie, who as Huntly's deputy took dire vengeance on the Forbeses for the deed. His eldest son, another Alexander of Abergeldie, engaged in the civil wars against the Covenanters, and in 1644 Abergeldie Castle narrowly escaped destruction on this account. A long line of Gordon lairds followed, down to modern times.

ABOYNE CASTLE

This great and famous house, now unhappily falling into ruin, stands within a large estate one mile north of the village of that name in the Dee valley. Long the seat of a senior branch of the House of Gordon, it still belongs to the Marquis of Huntly, Cock o' the North, who lives on the property nearby. It is a tall, impressive but rambling building of composite construction, dating from 1671, 1801 and 1869. The site was originally marshy and the castle was surrounded by a moat.

The north-west portion is the most ancient and was rebuilt by Charles Gordon, first Earl of Aboyne, uncle of the first Duke of Gordon. His initials and those of his wife, Elizabeth Lyon, c.g.e.a. and e.l.c.a. appear on the building. On the lintel of the old entrance is the sacred monogram i.h.s. and the date 1671. The structure has been so altered and added to that it is difficult to trace the original planning, but it is obviously grouped around the tall five-storey central tower, circular but corbelled out to the square at top, and crowned with the classical balustrade instead of the usual parapet. There are slender stair-turrets in the re-

entrants, topped by caphouses with ogee roofs. A similar tower at the north-eastern angle is a more modern replica. The gables are not crowstepped, and the windows throughout are large, as was usual for the period.

The property early belonged to the formerly powerful family of Bisset, passing in 1242 to the Knights Templar. By the early 15th century the Gordons of Huntly were in possession, with whose descendants it has remained. In 1836 a collateral, George, 5th Earl of Aboyne, succeeded the last Duke of Gordon as head of the Gordons and 9th Marquis of Huntly. The 1671 builder was the original hero of the ballad 'Lord Aboyne'. Aboyne Castle saw much stirring activity during the religious civil wars, and Argyll, the Covenanting leader, took it and made it his headquarters in 1640. We read that his men had a daily allowance off the country-side there of 24 bolls of meal, 120 sheep, a variable number of cattle and 60 dollars in cash.

ACHANACHIE CASTLE

Here is an unusual and interesting example of a small laird's house, dating from the late 16th and 17th centuries, situated near the Banffshire border five miles north-west of Huntly. The build-ing, now occupied by the farm grieve, shows extensive develop-

ments from the original tall and small-roomed tower, with some alterations, probably all having been reduced in height. A notable feature is the massive projecting and stepped chimney-stack midway along the east front of the main 17th-century extension. The fireplace for this, unfortunately, has been built-up internally. The walls are harled.

The tower is three storeys in height now, with a large circular stair-tower, almost certainly an addition, projecting in the re-entrant with the eastern extension, this being provided with tiny slit windows and a series of square shot-hole type apertures under the eaves, as at Aswanley not far away. A stone spout projects to carry off rain-water at the junction with the extension roof. Over the present doorway, beside the great chimney-stack, in the east front, is a panel inscribed FROM OVR ENEMIES DEFENDE VSOCHRIST 1594. This is probably re-inserted from the original doorway to the tower, which is now enclosed with later building.

The vaulted basement of the tower is particularly interesting in having three stone bosses dependant from the vault, carved with the arms of Gordon, Fraser and Campbell. The turnpike stair is very steep, and the tiny Hall on the first floor is unusual in being also vaulted. No other features of interest survive.

Achanachie was a Gordon house, like so many in this area, the dwelling of the eldest sons of the Gordons of Avochie. Strangely enough, Avochie Castle itself, now a fragmentary ruin and standing a few miles to the east, was a still smaller house than this. This family took an active part in most of the fighting of the troubled reigns of Mary Queen of Scots and of her son, James the Sixth, and later. In the early 17th century it passed to the second son of the 4th laird of Avochie, and remained thereafter with that branch of the family.

ARNAGE CASTLE

This attractive late 16th-century house stands in a fairly remote situation about five miles north of Ellon and two miles east of Shivas. Originally a comparatively small fortalice on the Z-plan, it has been restored and added to in modern times, unfortunately with rather unsightly enlargement of the first-floor windows. It is three storeys in height, with an extra storey contrived within the stair-wing. Two stair-turrets in the re-entrant angles carry up the stairs above first-floor level, and another tiny turret provides private access to garret level only. The walls of rough rubble and dressed quoins are well supplied with shot-holes, triple sets to the front and splayed type gunloops to the back.

The main block lies north and south, the stair-wing projecting to the south-east. The entrance, now built up, has been in the foot of this wing, protected by shot-holes and with two panel spaces above. The basement is vaulted and lit by slit windows, and the Hall, as usual, was on the first floor, with private accommodation above. A well, formerly enclosed within the courtyard, remains to the east.

The lands of Arnage came by marriage to the Cheyne family towards the end of the 14th century, and remained with them until sold in 1643. The house therefore was of their construction, and recent research has shown it to have been designed by the

celebrated master-mason Thomas Leiper, who was responsible for the handsome Castle of Tolquhon nearby. Of the Arnage family came James Cheyne, Rector of the Scots College at Douay, who died 1602. Another James, the last of the line, sold Arnage to John Sibbald, an elder of the kirk at Ellon, who, a few years later, perhaps on account of his aggrandisement to lairdship, was in trouble with the authorities for absenting himself from the kirk. In 1702 Arnage was bought by Bailie John Ross, later Provost of Aberdeen, for 40,000 merks. His grand-daughter married Alexander Leith of Freefield and their descendants took the name of Leith-Ross, retaining possession until recent times.

ASWANLEY

This interesting laird's house is situated in the Deveron valley, amongst pleasant foothill country, seven miles west of Huntly. A long low L-planned structure of two storeys and a garret, with a circular stair-tower projecting from the main block northwards, it was formerly enclosed on the south by a courtyard, the arched entrance for which still survives. This has a renewed pediment, initialled G.C. for George Calder and I.S. for Isobel Skene, daughter of Skene of Skene, and was erected in 1692.

The building which appears to date from the first half of the 17th century, has obviously suffered considerable alteration, and may have been smaller originally, with the western portion and the wing an early addition. The roof appears to have been lowered, while the circular stair-tower remains at its original height, giving a somewhat top-heavy appearance. This tower has a modern ogival roof added; its windows are small and it is provided with shot-holes. A later squared stair rises in the re-entrant angle. The walls are harled and yellow-washed.

The building is now used as a farmhouse, and little of interest remains internally. There is no vaulting, but the arch of the large kitchen fireplace is still traceable in what is now an internal dividing wall but which may have been the original west gable. The kitchen chimney-stack is notably massive.

First records of Aswanley make it a possession of the Cruickshanks family. Elizabeth Cruickshanks is reputed to have been mother to the famous illegitimate sons of the last of the true Gordons of Strathbogie, Jock of Scurdargue and Tam of Riven, or Ruthven, renowned in ballad. The father, Sir John Gordon, fell at Otterburn in 1388, and left as heiress his legitimate daughter,

[18]

another Elizabeth, who married Sir Alexander Seton of the Winton family. Their son took the name of Gordon and was created 1st Earl of Huntly, and from him the later Gordon chiefs descend. But it is from his illegitimate uncles that most of the numerous ancient Gordon lairdships of Aberdeenshire derive. In 1440 a Hugh Calder received a charter of Aswanley from Huntly. Twelve years later he accompanied the Earl to the Battle of Brechin, and thereafter is said to have followed Earl 'Beardie' Crawford home to Finavon Castle in disguise, and there stolen a silver drinking-cup which became a famous object of dispute. The last of the Calder lairds, a merchant in Aberdeen, died in 1768, in debt to Duff of Braco, ancestor of the Dukes of Fife, who thus obtained the property. Of the Aswanley family came Sir James Calder, created a baronet in 1686.

BALBITHAN HOUSE

This fine house in a lovely setting is especially interesting, for more reasons than one. Standing in a secluded valley two miles north-east of Kintore, it has attained a measure of fame as being the last of the tower-houses, the final fling of the fortified-house tradition, built as it were out of due time. Whether this is quite accurate, however, I think is open to question.

Balbithan is a handsome and commodious house on the L-plan, with an unusually wide stair-tower rising in the re-entrant, the upper portion of which was itself reached by a typical smaller turret stair. There are angle-turrets at the gables of each wing. The

[19]

walls are harled and cream-washed, there are no shot-holes or gunloops, and the gables have lost their crowstepping. Clearly the roof-level has been altered. The turrets project too high above the present roof—indeed they are now inaccessible from within—and the ceilings of the second-floor rooms have been raised. Also the turret stair comes to an abrupt end, leading to nowhere, and the head of the stair-tower has evidently been altered. Originally, almost certainly, this would contain the usual watch-chamber. There is an empty panel-space set above the corbelling of the stair-turret, and below is the main entrance, in the foot of the stair-tower. This is still provided with its long wooden bar, which slides into a deep socket in the walling when not in use. Traces of tempera wall-paintings have recently been uncovered, during restoration work.

Internally the planning is spacious and well-proportioned, none of the basement apartments being vaulted; this, together with the straight type of main stair, indicates a late date of construction. The east wall of the south wing is notably thick, however—thick enough to contain a mural staircase from the wine-cellar to the Hall above, plus wall-chambers, all highly unusual in late work. The first floor houses a fine Hall in the south wing, now the library, with a wall-chamber and aumbry as well as the aforementioned private turnpike stair. The west wing at this level contains two good public rooms, intercommunicating. Above is ample bedroom accommodation—although not so much as formerly, the roof lowering and ceiling raising no doubt doing away with an attic storey.

Most authorities describing this house have dated it as late as 1679, because this date appears on a metal sundial attached to the

south turret of the west wing, with the initials I.C. for James Chalmers. This sundial does not seem to be *in situ*, however, and need not relate to any building period. It is known that the Chalmers family who had been at Balbithan since before 1490, when the lands were still under the superiority of the Abbey of Lindores, removed their residence here from Old Balbithan on the bank of the Don over a mile away, for reasons of privacy, and it has been presumed that this occurred at or about 1679, because of the sundial and late features of the present house. However, there is much in the architecture of the south wing to suggest an earlier date, and the Register of the Great Seal refers to the Newbigging of Balbithan as early as February 1600. A charter of 1635 is given at the *novo loco de Balbithan*—the new place. A glance at the sketch will show that the two wings are by no means identical, as at first may appear, that to the south being plainer and more massive. It is in this south wing that the very thick walling, mural stairway and garderobes are to be found, and it seems likely that the original house on this site dates from the end of the 16th century, and that it was largely added to, in a similar style, and greatly altered internally, in the second half of the 17th century, with still later roof alteration.

At the Reformation, the Chalmers family, long in possession, no doubt obtained the superiority from Patrick Leslie, 1st Lord Lindores who had obtained the Abbey lands from the Crown. During their lairdships, which continued until 1690, they supplied many notable Aberdeenshire figures. Montrose and his colleagues made Balbithan a rendezvous during the Covenanting troubles. It is also said to have provided a refuge for Prince Charles' adherents after Culloden. After being sold by the Chalmers, Balbithan passed through various hands, including the families of Hay, Gordon and the Earl of Kintore. It is now, happily, in the possession of loving and appreciative proprietors, who are restoring it as far as possible to its former excellence.

BALFLUIG CASTLE

Balfluig, situated in the fertile Howe of Alford, a mile south-east of the village of Alford, is a modest-sized but tall laird's house of the late 16th century, fairly plain but with some interesting features, now unfortunately semi-ruinous. It conforms to a variation of the popular L-plan, with a wing projecting eastwards at the south end of the main block in such fashion as to form two re-

entrant angles, with a semi-circular stair-tower rising within the
outer angle, that facing south-west. The walls are of very rough
rubble and rise to three storeys and a garret in the main block, the
wing reaching a storey higher to finish in the usual watch-chamber. The roofing of the wing and stair-tower has been altered. The
outer angles of the masonry throughout are rounded, but corbelled to the square near roof-level; the stair-tower is also squared
at the top. A handsome and massive stepped chimney-stack rises
at the south gable of the main block. The walls are well supplied
with gunloops, of the rectangular variety, and slit windows. Three
external corbels on the east face at second-floor level, with two
doorways now built-up, reveal that there has been a defensive
timber hoarding here, a feature unusual in lesser castles. A courtyard lies to the east.

The entrance is in the main re-entrant, within the courtyard, by
a round-headed doorway, flanked by gunloops. The basement
contains two vaulted chambers in the main block, the kitchen to
the north with its 7 feet wide fireplace and sink and drain, the
wine-cellar to the south with its private stair to the Hall above.
There is a vaulted guardroom in the base of the wing, and a small
pit or prison has been contrived beneath the turnpike stairway.
The Hall on the first floor has a vaulted private room off—a somewhat unusual arrangement. The flooring of the upper rooms has
gone. There is a very narrow access stair to the watch-chamber
contrived at the head of the stair-tower.

Balfluig, in the centre of the Forbes country, belonged to a
branch of that great House, cadets of the Corsindae family. It was
the fortalice of the barony of Alford in 1650. There is a local tradition that there was at one time another fortalice sufficiently

nearby to occasion much mutual antipathy between the two lairds, who used to shoot at each other from their watch-chambers, one eventually managing to kill the other—the survivor repenting the deed for the rest of his life. Balfluig was sold to Farquharson of nearby Haughton in 1753.

BARRA CASTLE

Barra is assuredly one of the most attractive of the lesser castles of this great county. Although generally assumed to have been built in the early 17th century and added to a century later, there is probably an earlier nucleus, for the family of King lived here from the mid-13th century for 300 years. It stands at the western foot of Barra Hill, near where Bruce defeated the Comyn Earl of Buchan in 1307, two miles south-west of Old Meldrum, the main A.981 highway running close by. Backed by its farm-steading, it is an excellent example of a fortified laird's house.

The plan is a somewhat complicated variation of the L, with main block lying north and south and a wing projecting eastwards at the south end so as to form two re-entrants; in the other re-entrant is a circular stair-tower, corbelled out to the square at top to form the usual watch-chamber; and there are two more round towers, with conical roofs, projecting at the south-west corner of the main block and the south-east corner of the wing. The 18th-century addition extends eastwards at the north end of the main block,

thus forming three sides of a square, a curtain wall joining this and the wing to enclose a forecourt. The walls, of coursed rubble, are three storeys and a garret in height. The dates 1614 and 1618 appear on the upper part of the building.

The entrance is in the main re-entrant, within the courtyard, and at eaves level above is a crowstepped gablet—an unusual feature. The basement is vaulted and contains the customary kitchen and cellars. The turnpike stairway is unusually wide. The Hall on the first floor has been a fine apartment, subdivided at an early date to form dining and drawing-rooms, pine panelled, with a tiny chamber off, in the south-west tower. There is a bedroom at this level in the wing, also with a small chamber in the south-east tower. There is ample bedroom accommodation above and in the extension.

The Kings of Barra were long at feud with the Setons of Meldrum nearby, as a result of a King having slain a Seton in 1530 on the Braes of Bourtie. The feud might have been expected to be settled when, towards the close of the 16th century, James King sold Barra to a son of Seton of Meldrum. But no; as late as 1615, Elizabeth Seton pursued at law James King 'sumtyme of Barra' and others for being art and part in the slaughter of her father, Alexander, fiar of Meldrum, 'with schottis of hagbuttis and muscattis, committed upon the landis of Barra . . .'. The Setons did not long retain Barra, selling it in 1630 to James Reid. It would seem therefore that the Kings built the original house, and during their short ownership the Setons altered and added to it. The Reids held Barra until 1753, John Reid of Barra being created a baronet in 1703. Thereafter the property passed to the Ramsay family, who added the north-east extension in 1755. A Ramsay heiress early this century carried Barra to a cadet of the ancient family of Irvine of Drum, so that their descendants are still in possession.

BELDORNEY CASTLE

This substantial fortalice stands in a secluded position in the Deveron valley, amongst the hills two miles south of Glass and near to the Banffshire border. It belongs to the Z-plan, a main block lying approximately north and south, with a square stair-tower projecting to the north-west and a large round tower to the south-east. A tall, slender stair-turret rises above first-floor level in the re-entrant facing south-west between round tower and main block, and another, very tiny, is corbelled out between the

main gable and the stair-tower above second-floor level, to give
access to the watch-chamber in the top of the tower, which rises
a storey higher than the rest of the house. The walls are roughcast
and of three storeys. The round tower is encircled by two stringcourses and ends with a curious rounded gable. No gables are
crowstepped. There is a small late gablet surmounting the main
wallhead, facing west. The long stair-turret has a heraldic panel
set high, bearing the Gordon arms and initials. The stair-tower
has the representation of a dog perching on the summit of its west
gable. A later and lower wing has been thrust out westwards,
parallel with the stair-tower, to form a small paved entrance
courtyard enclosed by a wall and gateway. There is a modern
house attached, to the north.

The original entrance is to the west, within the courtyard, in
the foot of the stair-tower, and above are two empty panel-spaces.
There is a later door nearby and still another has been opened on
the east or garden front. The house is in process of being restored
by the present owners. The basement is vaulted and has contained
the kitchen. From one of the basement cellars a narrow private
stair rises to the Hall above. There is much pine panelling in the
house, and some good fireplaces.

Beldorney belonged to a branch of the great House of Gordon,
descended from Adam, third son of the 1st Earl of Huntly. In
1554 Gordon of Beldorney is recorded as buying the property of
Wester Fowlis from Huntly, but that date seems too early for the

present house, which would appear to date from the first half of the 17th century. The last of the Gordons, Charles, of Wardhouse, sold Beldorney in 1807.

BRAEMAR CASTLE

Braemar Castle is frequently considered to be merely a sham, because of its unsightly English-style crenellations and false-battlemented upper works. But if the top third of the building is ignored, it will be seen that the remainder is a typical L-planned Scots fortalice of the early 17th century, with a circular stair-tower in the re-entrant angle and angle-turrets on the corners.

It stands on the upper Dee about a mile north of Castleton of Braemar, and is surrounded by an 18th century defensive military wall, as at Corgarff. It was built, the last of the many castles of the Mar earldom, in 1628, by the 7th Erskine Earl, and despite its late date, was involved in much excitement. Here, in 1689 during the early Jacobite campaign of Viscount Dundee, it was held for the government by the Earl; but his death demoralised the garrison, and Farquharson of Inverey's Jacobites captured the castle. Here also 25 years leater, Bobbing John, the next Earl of Mar, raised the standard of revolt that began the Rising of 1715. At the close

of the Jacobite attempts, in 1748, the government took a long lease of the then semi-ruinous building from Farquharson of Invercauld who had bought it from the forfeited Mars, and turned it into a fortress-cum-barracks to aid in the subjection of the Highlands. Then it was that the unattractive tops were put on the tower and turrets.

There was also much internal alteration, but the vaulted basement chambers remain, and a fine iron yett still hangs at the stairfoot.

CAIRNBULG CASTLE

Standing not far from the sea, on a mound in lonely-seeming sandhill country two miles south-east of Fraserburgh, Cairnbulg is a large and impressive castle containing work of a very early date, but belonging mainly to the 14th, 15th and 16th centuries, with later additions and restorations. It consists of a tall and massive keep rising four storeys to a parapet, with garret storey above, attached by lower and later work to a round tower of the 16th century, substantial but a storey lower. This probably was originally a flanking tower. The building had fallen into a state of ruin in the late 18th century, but was restored in 1896.

The keep, oblong save for a small staircase wing, has harled walls, seven feet in thickness, rising to a renewed parapet carried on individual corbelling, with open rounds at all angles save the south-east where the walk is blocked by a gabled caphouse-cum-watch-chamber at the head of the stair-tower. This stair-wing is a 16th-century addition, although apparently the original stairway rose in the walling in the same angle. All above parapet level has been renewed. There is a machicolated projection at this level on the east front, to defend the original doorway beneath. The later door adjoins, at the foot of the stair-wing, not in the re-entrant.

The basement is vaulted, as is the Hall on the first floor. The Hall vault is 18½ feet high, and its fireplace 8 feet wide. The windows have stone seats, and that to the south-west gives access to a large L-shaped mural chamber in the thickness of the angle. There are other garderobes and aumbries. The floor above, now one chamber but formerly subdivided, is particularly interesting in that it has, in the south-west angle, a mural chamber large enough to hold a bed, and from which descends a small turnpike stair to a pit or prison in the thickness of the masonry—an unusual position for such amenity. There was a similar two-chamber floor above, and then the garret.

[27]

The round tower has a dome-vaulted basement, with apertures for three wide splayed gunloops. The room above is octagonal. All above has been modernised. The peculiar cylindrical battlemented top storey appears from early prints to be a reconstruction of the original: possibly it had a conical roof, as on the drum towers of Holyroodhouse. The lower work linking these two towers is a modern reconstruction of the ruined 16th century hall-house.

The first castle on the site seems to have been erected to guard the coast from Viking invaders, but the main mass of the present keep appears to date from the 14th century. Sir Alexander Fraser came north in 1375, marrying a daughter of the 5th Earl of Ross, and obtaining this barony of Philorth, he himself being linked with the royal house. No doubt he built the present keep. Cairnbulg remained in the possession of the powerful Frasers of Philorth for many centuries, and is still the seat of the head of that family, Lord Saltoun. For some generations however it was out of their hands, for in 1666 the then laird had to sell the castle, and built himself a new house at Philorth. He succeeded, through his mother two years later, as 10th Lord Saltoun. His descendant, the present 19th Lord, bought back Cairnbulg in 1934, after it had been restored by Mr John Duthie, his Philorth House having been burned down in 1915.

All this would seem pleasingly to fulfil the prophecy, imputed to the busy Thomas the Rhymer that:

> While a cock crows in the North,
> There'll be a Fraser in Philorth.

Unfortunately for the legend, however, True Thomas died a good 60 years before the first Fraser came to the North.

CORGARFF CASTLE

This much-altered but grimly impressive stronghold, now in the care of the Ministry of Works, stands in a lofty and remote position at the head of Strathdon, in a strategic site dominating the south end of the famous Lecht road through the hills to Tomintoul, near Cock Bridge. It is a tall tower of four storeys and a garret, oblong on plan, with its staircase carried a storey higher to form a caphouse at the south-east angle—an arrangement similar to that at Knock, and at Durris House in Kincardineshire. After the Rising of 1745, the Government took over Corgarff, turning it into a fort for the subjection of this area, much altering the structure, adding the two low wings and erecting round it the octangular loop-holed curtain-wall, similar to that built at Braemar Castle.

The original tower, of rough coursed rubble, appears to date

from the second half of the 16th century. It is now severely plain, with no other features than the gabled caphouse, but there are built-up small windows and loops, and at eaves level above the doorway on the south front are the corbels for a machicolated projection for the casting down of missiles upon attackers. There are indications that there may have been an angle-turret at the north-east corner. The gables are not now crowstepped and the regular placing of the later windows detracts from the authentic appearance.

The basement contains two plain vaulted cellars, formerly with no access save by a straight stair in the walling from above. The entrance is at first-floor level, now reached by a stone forestair to the south. A squared stair now rises to the right, in the south-east angle, to all floors, but this was originally a turnpike. The first floor was a single chamber, but was later subdivided. Since there appears to have been no basement kitchen, this floor presumably provided that necessary amenity, rather than the usual Hall. The second-floor chamber may therefore have been the Hall—but the interior of the castle was so altered for military purposes in the 18th century that little is to be gained by speculation.

Corgarff was part of the Earldom of Mar which was annexed by the Crown in 1435. James the Fourth granted it to the Elphinstones, and it seems probable that the fortalice was built when the lands were given by his father to the Master of Elphinstone at his marriage in 1546, for there is no mention of a fortalice earlier. The Erskine Earls of Mar recovered Corgarff in 1626, but it passed to the Forbeses after the forfeiture of Bobbing John, Earl of Mar, leader of the Rising of 1715. This was not the first Forbes interest in the place, for in 1607 the Master of Elphinstone complained to the Privy Council that on 14th May, at night, Alexander Forbes of Towie and sundry others of the clan came to his fortalice of 'Torgarffa and with grite geistis, foir-hammeris' and other instruments forcibly broke in, and fortified it as a house of war, assisted by Highland thieves and limmers. The Forbeses were denounced as rebels. Corgarff was burned by the Jacobites in 1689 in order to deny it to the Government, and again in 1716 by the Government as reprisal against Mar. It was however used again by the Jacobites in 1745. In 1571 it had been the scene of the famous tragedy of Edom o' Gordon.

CORSE CASTLE

Although now a roofless ruin, sufficient remains of Corse to prove that it has been a particularly interesting and well-built house of the late 16th century, on an unusual plan. It occupies a strong position above the Corse Burn, here dammed to form a small loch, three miles north-west of Lumphannan, the modern mansion standing nearby. Lofty, and constructed of warm red stone, the building conforms to an elaboration of the Z-plan, consisting of a rectangular main block lying north and south, with a square tower projecting to the south-east and a round tower, now almost wholly ruinous, to the north-west. In addition, there is a very tall circular stair-tower projecting to the south, carried up higher than the remainder of the wallhead, no doubt to contain a watch-chamber at the top—but this has not been corbelled out to the square as is usual. There are also angle-turrets remaining at the corners of the square tower and main block. The walls are pierced by the usual gunloops and shot-holes, and there are also tiny diamond-shaped windows, which may likewise have been used for defence.

The entrance is in the foot of the square tower, in the re-entrant and is surrounded by empty panel-spaces and a lintel with the initials w.f. for William Forbes, and e.s. for Elizabeth Strachan his wife, dated 1581. The interior in now wholly gutted and little of the lay-out can be traced. But one unusual feature is apparent;

owing to the falling away of the ground level, vaulted cellars were constructed only under part of the house. The great kitchen fireplace can be traced in the north gable of the main block. The usual arrangement of Hall on the first floor and sleeping accommodation above would apply.

The Forbes family of Corse was founded by Patrick, son of the 1st Lord Forbes, who died in 1448. A successor, William Forbes, whose former house had been plundered by Highland caterans, vowed: 'If God spares my life I shall build a house at which thieves will knock ere they enter.' This fortalice is the result. His son Patrick born 1564, succeeded in 1598, was a studious and pious young man but not bred for the Church. However, accustomed to read and expound the Scriptures to his own family, on the death of the local minister, and with no new incumbent forthcoming, he was induced to occupy the pulpit. This was condemned by Gledstanes, the Archbishop of St. Andrews. The Laird of Corse fought back, pointing out that at least 21 churches lay 'unplanted' in the two local presbyteries. Thereafter he entered the ministry officially, and was in 1618 appointed Bishop of Aberdeen, and Chancellor of King's College. Curiously enough his brother John also became a minister and in 1606 was Moderator of the Kirk, and, in opposition to episcopacy, was put to the horn—an intriguing situation for two brothers. Another brother went soldiering to Ireland and founded the Forbes family, Earls of Granard. Despite the door at which thieves would have to knock, the lands of Corse were still continually plundered by Highland raiders, and in 1638 they even carried off the laird's cousin, demanding a heavy ransom if his life was to be spared. Small wonder that fortified houses were still being erected in Aberdeenshire at the end of that century.

CORSINDAE HOUSE

Situated in pleasantly rural foothill country five miles west of Dunecht, Corsindae is a small but tall L-shaped tower-house of the 16th century, skilfully added to, and now, at first glance, appearing to be a much larger fortalice of unusual but homogeneous design. The original building appears to have consisted only of the projecting crowstepped-gabled wing seen to the left of the sketch, with a portion of the main block lying at right-angles to it. This may date from the early 16th century, or even earlier, for there is a charter of the property dated 1486. Then,

probably in the late 16th century, the left-hand circular stair-tower was added in the re-entrant angle. All the rest represents much later additions, however much of a piece it may seem under its harled and whitewashed exterior. Proof that the circular tower is not an original feature is provided by traces of an earlier outside door and small window built up behind it in the re-entrant. The present entrance, which leads into one of the two vaulted basement chambers, is not original therefore. Nor, of course, is the main block gablet above. The house is maintained in excellent order by appreciative owners.

Corsindae was a Forbes lairdship, the family descending from the 2nd Lord Forbes. In 1605 Alexander Irvine of Drum apprehended John Forbes of Corsindae, one of the 'insolent society of boyis denounced for slaughter and other enormities'. The Council charged the Earl Marischal to convey him to prison at Brechin, and a guard was sent all the way from Edinburgh to escort him thither—indicative of the power of the House of Forbes in this area.

CRAIG CASTLE

The Craig of Auchindoir, to give this castle its full name, is a massive and most interesting fortalice standing above a steep dean two miles north of Lumsden. With a more modern mansion attached, it is still occupied and in good condition.

The building has a number of unusual features, the most obvious being that although the wallhead has apparently been designed to finish with a parapet and open walk, in normal early fashion, a change of plan during construction has enclosed the parapet with an oversailing roof, out of which the crowstepped gables and chimney-stacks project strangely. The parapet-walks thus become roofed-in galleries. The castle belongs to the L-plan, with a main block lying approximately north and south and the wing projecting eastwards. The massive roughcast walls rise to four storeys, and are well provided with large and wide gunloops. The impression given is as plain as it is strong, save within the re-entrant angle. This is the entrance front, and there are a number of features. Here is the rounded moulded doorway surmounted by three heraldic panels, displaying the arms of Patrick, 1st Gordon laird, and his wife Elizabeth Stewart of Laithers, flanked by those of the 2nd and 3rd lairds, the last with the date 1548 carved in mixed numerals M.D. 4.8., and initials. The doorway is well protected with gunloops, and above is a large Hall window still retaining its handsome iron grille. Interesting is the way in which the section of the parapet above this front is built out on a quite elaborate corbel-table, leading to an angle-turret, with conical roof, at the south-east corner—an unexpected feature in a house of the early 16th century, and which may be a 17th-century addition.

A stout oak door two inches thick is reinforced by another heavy iron yett, and gives access to a vaulted vestibule and passage from which are entered two vaulted cellars in the main block and the kitchen in the wing; also, on the left, into a small guardroom from which is reached the pit or prison in the thickness of the 7-foot walling. The kitchen contains the usual arched fireplace, $8\frac{1}{2}$ feet wide, with an aumbry, probably for salt, at one side. The northern cellar was the wine-cellar, with its convenient private stair from the Hall above. The vestibule vaulting is handsomely groined.

The main turnpike stair at the end of the passage is of good width and rises to all floors. The Hall has been a fine apartment 29 by 18 feet, but has latterly been partitioned off to form closets at the north end. The 7-foot wide fireplace has been shortened, and other alterations made. There is a private room in the wing, and a small bedroom has been contrived in the walling between. There has been a gallery in the thickness of the north wall, open-

[34]

ing on to the Hall, either as a minstrels' gallery or a chapel where the priest could be observed from the Hall below. The second floor has contained an Upper Hall now subdivided, plus private room, and a long narrow mural chamber in the east wall. Higher were attic bedrooms.

There is a courtyard to the east, entered by a handsome gateway dated 1726, with the arms of Francis Gordon, 8th laird, and the initials of all three of his wives along with his own.

The first Gordon of Craig was a grandson of the famous Jock o' Scurdargue, and the castle was presumably built immediately after he obtained the lands in 1510, for he is said to have died at Flodden. His grandson, another Patrick, was killed at Pinkie, and *his* son, William, was implicated with his chief, Huntly, in the murder of the Bonnie Earl of Moray at Donibristle in 1592. So the tale goes on, one laird after another involved in the successive troubles of the times right down to 1863 when the last of the line, an heiress, was burned to death with her daughter at Nice. The lands were sold in 1892 to the present owners.

CRAIGIEVAR CASTLE

Set in an isolated wooded situation amongst the Grampian foot-hills, five miles north of Lumphannan, Craigievar is of course one of the most deservedly renowned 17th-century castles in all Scotland. The property belonged to the Mortimer family from 1457 until 1610, and it was at the very end of this period that one of them began to build the present castle, but had to give up for lack of funds. The estate was sold to William, second son of Forbes of Corse, nearby, and brother of the celebrated Patrick, Bishop of Aberdeen, who, 'by his diligent merchandising in Denmark and other parts had become extraordinary rich'. He finished the build-ing in 1626 in a style which splendidly displays the full flowering of the Scottish castellated architecture allied to the lighter French influence. Constructed of warm pink-harled granite, rising to seven storeys, and finishing in a rich cluster of turrets, gablets, chimney-stacks and corbelling, it makes a most handsome house, with strong affinities with Castle Fraser, Crathes and Midmar Castles, not far off. Like Crathes, the external wall-corners are rounded off.

The plan, despite the elaborate aspect, is a comparatively simple one, of an L with a square tower in the re-entrant; all the elabor-ation is confined to the upper storeys, the lower walling being

entirely plain. The tower in the re-entrant contains the doorway, as is usual, but does not house a stairway, containing only a vestibule at basement level which gives access to three vaulted chambers, and to a straight stair in the centre of the house, which rises to the first floor only. This tower is crowned by a lofty balustraded parapet enclosing a flat roof, with a caphouse having an ogee roof. A handsome heraldic panel surmounts the doorway, at second-floor level.

Internally Craigievar is equally interesting. The Hall, which with a withdrawing-room occupies the first floor, is a magnificent vaulted apartment, with mixed groined and barrel vaulting most handsomely plastered. It retains its oak-panelled screens at the east end to form a service lobby. Behind this screen is a little pantry, a private stair down to the wine-cellar, and access to small minstrel galleries to the east. There is a large and notable fireplace with ornamental stone carving, and the royal arms in a panel above.

Higher is a profusion of private rooms, reached by no fewer than five turret stairways. Many of these rooms are panelled.

Craigievar stood formerly within a barmekin or curtain-wall, with round towers at the angles, one of which remains.

The son and namesake of the builder was a zealous Covenanter and responsible for the putting down of Gilderoy the freebooter and his band, and having them hanged in Edinburgh. He commanded a troop of horse in the Civil War, was Sheriff of Aberdeen, and was granted 16,000 acres of land in New Brunswick. He sat as M.P. from 1630 to 1646 and was created a Baronet of Nova Scotia in 1630. His great-grandson Sir William married the Hon. Sarah Sempill, eldest daughter of the 12th Lord Sempill, and their grandson succeeded as 17th Baron. Craigievar continued to be the seat of the Lords Sempill. It is now the property of the National Trust for Scotland.

CRAIGSTON CASTLE

This most unusual and impressive fortalice stands within its wooded estate about four and a half miles north-east of Turriff. It is particularly interesting for a number of features, and in that it is still in the hands of the Urquhart family, one of whose members built it in 1607. It is a lofty and commodious house on the E-plan, consisting of a main block lying north and south, with two wings projecting westwards, these linked in highly unusual fashion at

fourth-floor level with an archway supporting an ornate balcony. The elaborate corbelling for square angle-turrets projects at each outer angle, but it appears that the turrets themselves were never constructed. The roofing is gabled, with a peculiar flat-topped and balustered caphouse rising above all, like the summit of a square tower. The walls are harled, rising to five storeys and a garret, and the method of picking out the angles with lengthy separate quoins is highly individual. A later porch blocks the bottom of the high recess between the two wings, obscuring the original doorway.

The stonework of the corbelling, with its grotesque figures, is notable, and bears some resemblance to that of Balbegno in Kincardineshire. The underside of the arch linking the wings has been painted in tempera—another most unusual feature for outside masonry. Heraldic and decorative panels enhance the wings, above basement level, that on the left bearing the arms of John Urquhart, Tutor of Cromarty, the builder of the house; that on the right declaring: THIS VARK FOUNDIT YE FOURTENE OF MARCH ANE THOUSAND SEX HOUNDER FOUR YEIRIS AND ENDIT YE 8 OF DECEMBER 1607.

Internally the house is very fine, and in excellent preservation, with an abundance of splendid carved woodwork and panelling. The basement is vaulted, The Hall on the first floor measured 30 by 21 feet, and although most of its woodwork is of the 18th century, inserted is a unique series of carved oak panels of the early 17th century, representing Biblical notables and virtues. Of particular interest is the long gallery, housing a magnificent library, which runs along the front of the house at fourth-floor level—that is, above the arch and linking the two wings.

John Urquhart, the builder, was the uncle and Tutor of Sir Thomas Urquhart of Cromarty, father of the famous 17th-century 'character' the Cavalier Sir Thomas, translator of *Rabelais*, and author of no fewer than 128½ folio quires of manuscript, who professed, in his Genealogy to chronicle his descent from Adam, in grandiloquent fashion. The great-grandson of John Urquhart of Craigston sold the property, but a century later it was bought back by another remarkable representative of the line, Captain John Urquhart, known as The Pirate, born 1696, a Jacobite, who had a narrow escape from death at Sheriffmuir.

DAVIDSTON HOUSE

The attractive and interesting laird's house of Davidston, now a farm tenement, is remotely situated at the very north-western edge of the county, where the Burn of Davidston forms part of the boundary with Banffshire, about nine miles north-west of Huntly. The name is thought to derive from David, one of the early lords of Strathbogie, in which great area this property is included.

It is an L-shaped house of three storeys, dating from the 17th century, with main block lying approximately north and south, and the wing projecting westwards, circular angle-turrets gracing the north-east and south-west corners. The masonry is very rough local rubble, not so much harled as mortared over in patches, the crowstepping and corbelling being crude but effective. A number of windows have been built up and others enlarged, and a modern doorway has been opened in the south front of the wing. Under the north-east turret is carved a grinning face, dated 1678, with the inscription I.G AND T.A. BUILDED THIS HOUSE. There is another mask beneath the south-west turret, and there are weather-worn initials on a tiny lintel to a built-up square shot-hole window at basement level on the main east front.

Internally no features of any interest appear to have survived the various alteraltions, and the fabric is not now in the best of condition. The basement is not vaulted.

The initials referred to belong to the families of Gordon and

[39]

Abercrombie. It may be that the Gordon here referred to had married the Abercrombie heiress, and either built anew or much altered the house at this date.

DELGATIE CASTLE

This imposing castle stands on the flank of a valley, above a small loch, two miles east of Turriff, and is famous as an ancient seat of the great family of Hay, Earls of Erroll, High Constables of Scotland. It consists of a lofty keep of five storeys and a garret, with an uncrenellated parapet and open rounds 66 feet above the ground, dating probably from the 15th century—although there may well be older work included. To the west of this has been attached an equally tall late 16th century gabled house, and later and lower buildings now extend to east, west and north, not enhancing the aspect. The walls are exceedingly thick, harled and whitewashed, the original windows are small, and there are sundry gunloops and heraldic panels. The parapet is borne on a corbel-table of individual members between cable-mouldings.

The original entrance was in the west front, now obscured by the 16th-century addition, but the present modern porch to the south gives access to its entrance lobby, with a good ribbed and groined vault. From here a passage leads to the turnpike stairway which rises in the south-west angle of the keep. The old kitchen occupies the basement, and is vaulted, with the usual wide fireplace. The Hall above, a fine chamber, is also ribbed and groin-vaulted, the ribs splaying from corbels in the angles, the vault's apex boss being decorated in colour with the Hay arms. The wide fireplace lintel is dated 1570 and inscribed MY HOYP IS IN YE LORD. The building is well supplied with garderobes and mural chambers. Amongst the notable features is the tempera-painted ceiling on the second floor.

The castle is lovingly cared for, and its heraldic and other decoration skilfully enhanced by the present laird, Captain John Hay of Hayfield, Commissioner to the Constable, the Countess of Erroll.

Delgatie's history, being so closely linked with that of one of the most prominent and necessarily warlike families in the land, is as lengthy as it is stirring, but not to be recounted here. I content myself with two mentions. Mary Queen of Scots spent three days here after the Battle of Corrichie, on her single progress into the North to put down the power of Gordon. And Hay of Delgatie was standard-bearer to the great Montrose in 1645. At the defeat of Philiphaugh he became detached from his leader, with the standard; but, though thought to be a prisoner, or dead, he eventually found his way, after many adventures, to Montrose's castle of Buchanan, with the standard still safe.

DRUM CASTLE

The famous and splendid castle of Drum, in many ways one of the most interesting in the land, stands in a great estate on rising ground above the Dee three miles west of Peterculter. Besides being, in its original portion, one of the oldest occupied houses in Scotland, it has the added distinction of having been held by the same family since, in 1323, King Robert the Bruce gave a charter of the royal Forest of Drum to his faithful secretary and armour-bearer William de Irvine.

The castle is large, but the work of various periods is fairly easily defined. The original structure is the massive and dominant late 13th or early 14th-century tower which projects from the north-east angle of the quadrangular range of building, a plain keep of four main storeys beneath a parapet borne on individual corbels and having heightened open rounds at all angles. The roof is now flat but no doubt was originally gabled to contain the usual garret storey. The masonry, twelve feet thick at base, rounded somewhat at the angles, is of massive but mellow pink granite coursed rubble, and the windows, save for the few modern enlargements, are very small. There are sundry gunloops and arrow-slits. The stone forestair to the first-floor doorway is of course modern, and would replace the usual timber removable stairway.

Internally, the vaulted basement, lit only by slits, is reached by a straight stair in the walling from the first floor. The Common Hall, on the first floor, is also barrel-vaulted and probably has contained an entresol or half-floor. A newel-stair rises in the thickness of the south-east angle. The second floor housed the private Hall, larger than below because of a thinning of the walls to nine feet. This has a pointed barrel-vault, with corbels for an entresol floor still in place. It has windows with stone seats, a garderobe and large fireplace. The stair to the upper floors is of timber.

The very large additions were mainly erected in 1619, which date is carved in several places. It comprises an L-shaped range, of three storeys and a garret, harled, with square gabled projecting towers at the outer angles and a circular stair-tower rising to the south-west. Another smaller addition projects from the keep at the north-west, and more modern work extends this wing westwards. The courtyard thus formed is completed by a curtain-wall to the west, and is entered from a pend to the north.

There is no space here to detail the arrangements in the fine 17th-century house. Entering from the courtyard a wide straight

stair rises to the west, while a long corridor gives access to the
five vaulted basement chambers, including the kitchen with great
fireplace. There are also small vaulted rooms in the bases of the
square towers. There is another large Hall on the first floor, with
withdrawing-room to the east. This Hall has a private stair down
to the west tower room and an outside door—an unusual arrangement. The upper floor bedrooms are reached by several small
turnpike stairs.

The long history of the Irvines of Drum is full of incident and
colour. The original William was of the chiefly House of Bonshaw
in Annandale. The lairds of Drum ever took a notable part in the
stirring affairs of the North-East, being much involved with
feuding with Keiths and Forbeses. William's grandson, Sir Alexander, commanded and fell at the Battle of Harlaw in 1411, and
another Sir Alexander, the 13th, was the Laird o' Drum of the old
ballad. The builder of the 17th-century addition was a patron of
learning and donor of several bursaries to Marischal College,
Aberdeen. The present laird is a direct descendant.

DRUMINNOR CASTLE

This fine house, once the original seat of the Lords Forbes, has
recently come back to a descendant of that great family in the
person of the Honourable Miss Margaret Forbes-Sempill, who is

[43]

splendidly and painstakingly restoring the handsome building to its former aspect. The castle stands on a dramatically sloping site at the side of a steep valley, in foothill country two miles south-east of Rhynie in Upper Strathbogie. Although an early castle stood on this site, the oldest remaining part of the present building dates from 1440, but it was in 1577 that Druminnor gained the stair-tower and upper storeys which gave it its present distinctive aspect. There were further alterations in 1660, and in 1825 a wing was added at the north-west angle, now demolished, to the improvement of the building's authentic character.

The structure follows the L-plan, with a long main block lying east and west, and a circular stair-tower projecting northwards at the east end, corbelled out to the square at top to form a gabled watch-chamber. A slender stair-turret rises within the re-entrant above first-floor level. Because of the steeply-sloping site, the castle appears to be very tall from the south, and comparatively short, with only two storeys, an attic and a garret, from the north. The walls are rough-cast, pink-washed, and well supplied with gunloops.

The entrance is unusual in two ways. It is not within the re-entrant, but set in the front of the stair-tower; also its arched head is contrived out of five straight sections of moulding. Above are three Forbes heraldic panels, dated 1577, and there are wide flanking gunloops. The doorway midway along the north front is modern. The window in the west gable at semi-subterranean

level is still provided with its iron yett and has a shot-hole beneath. The walling is intaken slightly at first-main-floor level, no doubt where the 15th-century work ends.

The interior is still in process of restoration, and it is quite impossible here to do justice to Miss Forbes-Sempill's devoted and arduous work, or the most interesting nature of her discoveries, in the fabric. All the basements are vaulted. Basins and drains have been uncovered, both for the intake of water from the outside, and the disposal of slops from within, with garderobe shutes linked to the latter. The former kitchen, with its great arched fireplace, is now the dining-room. In the vaulted chamber next door, at main basement level, is an interesting inscription over the fireplace A HAPPY ROOM 144? I.R. (this last presumably for King James the Second). The main turnpike stair is of notable width—almost six feet. The Great Hall on the first floor is a handsome apartment, the ceiling here having been heightened. Fifteen Gordons are reputed to have been put to death by Forbeses in this room, at a banquet.

The author much regrets that space forbids the recording of further details.

This was the original Castle Forbes, and the scene of many stirring episodes in the turbulent history of the chiefs of that powerful Aberdeenshire family—the more so in that they were constantly at feud with the even larger clan of Gordon. Lord Forbes was a peer of Scotland before 1441. In 1571 was fought the Battle of Tillyangus, two miles away, over the repudiating by the Master of Forbes of his wife, elder daughter of the Earl of Huntly. The Gordons had the best of this encounter, Black Arthur, brother of Lord Forbes, being slain by William Gordon of Terpersie, and the Gordons pursued the defeated Forbeses to the gates of Druminnor. The aforementioned banquet is alleged to have taken place in 1571 also, presumably before the battle. To even list other major stirring events connected with this ancient house and its owners would entail cataloguing the history of the North-East of Scotland.

CASTLE FRASER

This is one of that splendid group of great houses of the late 16th and early 17th centuries for which this area is so justly famed, which includes Midmar, Craigievar, Crathes and Fyvie. Possibly Castle Fraser is the finest of them all—though some may choose

otherwise. This automatically places it high indeed in the proud
hierarchy of Scotland's castles. However, the main block includes
a nucleus of a simple 15th-century keep, so the building is not
quite what it seems.

The great house stands in a large estate in rolling country three
miles south of Kemnay. It is a tall and massive structure on the
Z-plan, with a main block of double width lying east and west,
with towers projecting at opposing angles, square to north-west,
round to south-east. Two long but lower wings project to form a
courtyard to the north, this being closed by subsidiary buildings
and an arched gateway.

The main fortalice is four storeys and an attic in height, with
the great round tower rising two storeys higher, to finish in a flat
roof with balustraded parapet, reached by a slender stair-turret
topped by an ogee-roofed and arcaded caphouse. The other
angles of main block and square tower are crowned by two-
storeyed angle-turrets borne on elaborate corbelling and amply
provided with lozenge-shaped shot-holes. The upper storeys of
the main block and both towers are projected on handsome continuous corbelling, and provided with dormer windows with
decorative pediments and many dummy cannon-like spouts. The
walls, of light-coloured coursed granite rubble in the main house,

but roughcast on the round tower, are well supplied with gun-loops, arrow-slits and triple shot-holes. The present handsome doorway is in the centre of the south front, but the original entrance was in the re-entrant of the square tower to north-west. High over the present doorway are three panels, one bearing the Royal Arms of Scotland and dated 1576; another dated 1683; and the third inscribed ELIZA FRASER 1795.

As usual the basement contains the vaulted kitchen and cellars. The wide turnpike stair rises, near the original entrance, to the first floor only, above which are smaller turret stairways. The Great Hall and principal apartments are on the first floor, and from these two private stairs lead down to the cellarage below. From one of the Hall windows a laird's lug or secret listening device communicates with a wall-closet entered from a bedroom above. Ample sleeping accommodation is contained in the upper storeys.

The two northern wings are of two storeys only, and each ends in a three-storey circular tower with conical roof. These subsidiary wings, are dated 1617, with a panel bearing the name of I. Bell. This was one of the great family of master-masons, responsible for Midmar etcetera. Almost certainly he built not only these wings but the handsome upper storey of the main house with all the magnificent detail.

It seems, therefore, that there was originally a plain 15th-century keep, which was added to in the 16th century to form a Z-plan castle, and then was heightened, embellished and extended in the early 17th century.

Originally known as Muchals-in-Mar, to distinguish it from Muchalls Castle in Kincardineshire, the Frasers in 1454, by a charter of James Second exchanged their lands of Cornton near Stirling for Muchals and Stoneywood in Aberdeenshire. In 1633 Alexander Fraser of Muchals was created Lord Fraser. The family took the Covenanting side, and suffered in consequence, Castle Fraser being spoiled by Montrose in 1644. At the 4th Lord's death in 1720 the title became dormant. The Frasers of Inverallochy, related, succeeded, but being Jacobites did not claim the title from the authorities. Charles Fraser commanded the clan contingent at Culloden. It was his neice Eliza whose name appears on the panel, who inherited, and dying in 1814 ended the main line of the Frasers of Castle Fraser.

FYVIE CASTLE

One of the best known and most splendid castles in all Scotland, Fyvie stands within a wooded park in the valley of the Ythan, a mile north of the village. It has been an important place from time immemorial, being a seat of the ancient Celtic church, a royal demesne, the capital messuage of the Thanage of Formartyne. It was granted by Robert the Second to his eldest son, the Steward of Scotland, later Robert the Third. When it passed out of royal hands in the late 14th century, Fyvie went through five periods of ownership, each of approximately a century, by the families of Preston, Meldrum, Seton, Gordon and Leith, and each has left tangible memorial in stone on the great house—although the most magnificent contribution was made in the period 1596 to 1622, by Alexander Seton, 1st Earl of Dunfermline, Chancellor of the realm and one of the great builders of Scotland.

The castle occupies a postion of strength on a sort of wide terrace above loch and river. It now comprises a great L, the wings being no less than 147 and 136 feet long, the principal front, with its handsome linked drum-tower entrance, known as the Seton Tower, facing south. Three other great towers, built by different families, rise at the angle of the L and the two extremities, the Preston, Meldrum and Gordon Towers, each similar in style but differing in detail, with rich corbelling, angle-turrets, steep crow-stepped roofs and dormer windows. Fyvie is indeed altogether too large, complex and full of feature to describe in any detail here, replete as it is with every development and refinement of the authentic Scottish baronial architecture, heraldic decoration and statuary enrichment.

The interior is as magnificent as the exterior, its great main newel stairway, 9 feet wide with 66 steps, decorated with 22 coats-of-arms, being one of the architectural glories of Scotland. The basement of the house is vaulted, with both barrel and groined vaults; many of the upper rooms and galleries are handsomely panelled in wood, painted in tempera and with magnificent plaster ceilings; and everywhere is a wealth of heraldic emblems, in wood, plaster and stone. To describe Fyvie adequately would fill a book —as indeed has been done in A. M. W. Stirling's *Fyvie Castle*.

Its history, naturally, is as resounding as the rest. William the Lion held court here in 1214 and Alexander the Second in 1222. Edward, Hammer of the Scots, visited 'Fyvin Chastel' in 1296. The Lady Margaret Keith, daughter of the Earl Marischal and wife to Robert the Third's cousin the Earl of Crawford, was be-

sieged in Fyvie by her own nephew Robert Keith, but relieved by her husband. Montrose occupied the castle in 1644, the ditches of his entrenched camp still to be seen on the high ground to the east. His great enemy Argyll attacked him here, in what was known as the Skirmish of Fyvie, but without success, though greatly superior in numbers. In 1646 the castle was fortified in the royalist interest by the Earl of Aboyne. Later again a Cromwellian detachment garrisoned Fyvie.

The castle is now the seat of the Forbes-Leith family.

GLENBUCHAT CASTLE

Standing on an eminence overlooking the confluence of the Water of Buchat and the Don, three miles north-east of Strathdon, Glenbuchat is a very handsome fortalice of the late 16th century, long a roofless ruin but complete to the wallhead and now in the care of the Ministry of Works. It is a Z-planned building of considerable extent, consisting of a main block lying east and west, with large square towers projecting to north-east and south-west, and formerly having a courtyard to the south. In the two re-entrants facing north-west fairly large stair-turrets rise above first-floor level, supported on squinches—an unusual feature in this area. Angle-turrets grace the wallheads, square and gabled at the south-east corner of the main block and south-west corner of the north tower; circular at the south-east angle of the south tower and

north-east corner of the north tower. The walls, of roughly coursed rubble, have dressed quoins, and rise to three storeys and a garret, being liberally supplied with shot-holes—some of which are contrived in the corbelling of the turrets for downward shooting. The west gable of the main block has an unusually large window for the Hall on the first floor, and a double window above.

The entrance is in the south tower, in the courtyard re-entrant, and above is a weatherworn lintel inscribed: NOTHING ON ARTH REMAINIS BOT FAIME. JOHN GORDONE—HELEN CARNEGE 1590. A guardroom lies nearby in the foot of the tower. The basement is vaulted, the kitchen with a very large fireplace occupying the main block, along with the wine-cellar with its private stair to the Hall above. The wide curving stairway appears to waste considerable space on the first floor. Here the Hall has been subdivided into dining and withdrawing-rooms, with a private bedroom for the laird opening off the latter in the north tower. The two turret stairs ascend hereafter to bedroom accommodation.

This Gordon fortalice in Forbes country housed one of the most powerful branches of the clan, descendants of Jock o' Scurdargue and the Rothiemay family—reputed to be a handsome and gallant race of men. Best known is the famous Jacobite Brigadier-General Gordon of Glenbuchat, one of the few leaders of that cause to be 'out' in both 1715 and 1745 and to escape the direst consequences. His spirited adventures on Prince Charlie's behalf are well known, when he was on the Prince's council and colonel of his regiment, leading the Gordons and Farquharsons at Culloden. He escaped

to France, where he did not die until a great age—to the distress
of his unacknowledged monarch German George, who is said
frequently to have wakened in the night sweating and trying to
pronounce the name of Glenbuchat, accompanied by exclamations
of terror. The Glenbuchat lands were forfeited, and later bought
by the acquisitive Duff Earl of Fife.

HALLHEAD

This small laird's house, set at the end of a long cart-track amidst
remote upland country five miles north-east of Tarland, is now a
farmhouse. Nevertheless it was the cradle of an important branch
of the great House of Gordon, that of Hallhead and Esslemont,
now Wolrige-Gordon. The simple T-planned structure has a main
block of two storeys and an attic, with a stair-tower projecting
centrally eastwards, and rising a storey higher to contain at the
top a watch-chamber reached by a small turret stair corbelled out
in the north-east re-entrant. The walls are harled, the gables crowstepped, the dormer pediments are modern, and the corbelling of
the stair-turret appears to have been plastered over in unsightly
fashion. The door is in the south-east re-entrant and has a moulded
surround. There are no shot-holes visible, although some might
be hidden behind the harling, for one is built into the wall of a
coachhouse, dated 1703, which has been part of the former courtyard.

Internally the house has been altered to suit present requirements. There is no vaulting.

Although the Gordons acquired Hallhead towards the end of the 14th century, the present house is said to have been built by the 9th laird in 1686. The 1st laird was George Gordon, fourth son of the famous Tam o' Riven, Sir Thomas Gordon of Ruthven, in Strathbogie, who, with his equally famous brother, Jock o' Scurdargue, represented albeit in bastardy, the original line of the Gordons of Strathbogie, when the legitimate heiress, Elizabeth, married Sir Alexander Seton and founded the chiefly Huntly line. A later George Gordon of Hallhead was out with Prince Charles Edward, and his town house in Aberdeen was plundered by the Duke of Cumberland. Descendants of the same family, although latterly in the female line, have held the property, with Esslemont, down to the present day.

HARTHILL CASTLE

Although ruinous, Harthill is comparatively well-preserved and an excellent example of a commodious Z-planned tower of the early 17th century. It stands on level ground above a burn, to the north of Benachie, one mile east of Oyne. The interesting remains of a gatehouse and part of an enclosing wall remain.

A tall main block lies north and south, four storeys and a garret in height, with a square tower projecting to the north-east and a round tower to the south-west. Corner-turrets grace the angles, and the walls, of granite rubble with dressed quoins, are well provided with gunloops. The entrance, in the main re-entrant angle, is by a moulded doorway, still provided with a deep socket for a sliding bar, and having an empty panel-space above.

The basement is vaulted. To the right of the doorway, in the base of the square tower, is a guardroom with ornate gunloops and slits guarding the entrance. The main stair rises alongside. The kitchen occupies the north of the main block basement, with large arched fireplace taking up the northern gable, provided with its own shot-hole. There is a service window to the lobby, a water-supply trough fed from a gutter outside, and also a stone sink and drain. Both this kitchen and the wine-cellar next to it have service stairs to the Hall above, and from the latter a peculiar slantwise shot-hole guards the west front. There is a dome-vaulted cellar in the foot of the round tower.

The Hall on the first floor is a fine apartment reached from the wide main turnpike stair through a window recess. It has a large fireplace with decorated jambs, with stone seats and a salt-box in

the ingoings. A door, now built up, opened on to the former parapet-walk of the courtyard wall, leading to the gatehouse. There are private rooms in the two towers, and ample further bedroom accommodation on the floors above, reached by turnpike stairs in the thickness of the north-east and south-west angles of the main block.

The gatehouse, over an arched entrance to the courtyard rests on an elaborate corbel-table. It is a small place, now represented only by a gable with a window flanked by two empty panel-spaces.

Harthill is usually said to have been built by Patrick Leith, a cadet of Leith-hall or Edingarroch, in 1638; but its appearance suggests a somewhat earlier date. The first Leith of Harthill had a charter from James Fifth in 1531. His great-grandson, Patrick, was the Young Harthill of the civil war period, noted for his bravery and leadership in the army of Montrose. He was captured by Middleton, and beheaded in 1647 at the age of twenty-five. His brother John inherited the estate, also a royalist but of a different temperament. It is recorded that once entering St. Nicholas' Church, Aberdeen, during mid-service, he insisted on taking the Provost's pew. On being offered another seat he drew sword and swore 'By God's wounds I'll sit beside the Provost and in no other place!' On being jailed, at his trial he asserted that the Provost was a 'doittit cock and ane ass', snatching the complaint from the clerk-of-court, tearing it up, and casting the inkhorn and penholder in the unfortunate clerk's face and 'thereby hurt and wounded him in two several parts to the great effusion of blood'. Whilst new proceedings were being arranged he tried to set the jail on fire, managed to arm the other prisoners, and fired on the populace. This awkward customer seems to have been eventually overcome—but was released in nine months when Montrose again gained mastery in Scotland. Four generations later the last laird is said to have been on such ill terms with all his neighbours that he at length set fire to Harthill and left Scotland, dying a pauper in London. The estate passed to the Erskines of Pittodrie.

HUNTLY CASTLE

Huntly, or Strathbogie, is one of the most celebrated castles in all Scotland, with one of the stormiest histories. Now consisting only of the great keep, its ruins are still highly impressive, in their strong position above the junction of the Rivers Bogie and Deveron just north of the town. The present structure, although at first glance homogeneous, dates from three periods, even the oldest portion of which represents only the second castle on the site. The original Strathbogie rose on a mound to the west and was a motte-and-bailey castle, mainly of timber and earthworks, built by the Celtic Earls of Fife. This early stronghold was burned down in 1452 by the Douglas Earl of Moray; the earliest part of the present fortalice dates from immediately thereafter.

Descendants of the Celtic lords took the wrong side in the War of Independence, and Bruce conferred their lands on Sir Adam Gordon, of Huntly in Berwickshire. The Border Gordons settled down in the north-east and speedily became powerful. Sir John Gordon in 1408 was succeeded by his sister Elizabeth whose husband, Sir Alexander Seton, took the name of Gordon, and was in 1436 created Lord Gordon. His son was the 1st Earl of Huntly. He built the oldest part here described.

This is a great oblong keep 76 feet by 36, lying east and west, with a large round tower 38 feet in diameter at the south-west. There is a smaller circular tower at the opposite north-east corner, but this was not original. A great courtyard and subsidiary building lay to north and east.

Huntly Castle was so often involved in war and rebellion, and supposedly razed to the ground, that it is frequently assumed the present building must date from later than the last, great casting-down, by James the Sixth in 1594. This is not so, for the total demolition of these enormously strong stone castles was seldom a

practical proposition. In this case the basement dates from 1452, the main part above from 1553, and only the top storey with all its elaborate stone-work, plus the smaller round tower, from after 1594. The lower storeys show the typical massive building of early castles, in rough coursed rubble, while the top is highly decorative and imaginative in dressed freestone, especially the south front which is enhanced with three handsome oriel windows on the main block and one seeming to cling to the round tower, with other windows, stringcourses, dormer pediments, heraldry and stone lettering flanking them. I have not shown this aspect in the sketch, for it is so well known, it gives a rather false impression of the strength of the castle, and it does not show the magnificent doorway and heraldic work of the smaller north-east tower—one of the finest doorways in the land.

This tower and doorway, erected by the 5th Earl and 1st Marquis dates from 1602, but a stairway and door must always have been in this position. A straight stair leads down to the four vaulted basement cellars, that in the great round tower being a singularly horrible pit or prison, mainly subterranean. The floor above, really at ground level, is also vaulted, containing two cellars flanking the kitchen, and a bedroom with garderobe in the round tower. Two turnpike stairs lead up from this bedroom, one to the first floor, the other right to the roof.

The Hall on the main first floor was a magnificent chamber 57 by 25 feet, now subdivided and its fireplaces torn out. A handsome fireplace still remains, however, in the great private room above, dated 1606. The round tower rises a storey higher, and is finished with a parapet carried on elaborate corbelling. There has been a conical roof within the parapet-walk, to which a pentagonal caphouse gives access.

Space forbids any further description or history of this great castle of the Cocks o' the North, now in the care of the Ministry of Works.

KEITHHALL OR CASKIEBEN

This interesting 'Jekyll and Hyde' mansion stands in a large wooded estate one mile east of Inverurie, and is the seat of the Earl of Kintore. Now known as Keithhall, its name was changed from Caskieben in 1662 when the property was purchased from the last of the Johnstons of Caskieben by Sir John Keith, third son of the 6th Earl Marischal, who was in 1677 created Earl of Kintore and Baron Keith of Inverurie and Keithhall, supposedly for services he rendered in the saving of the Scottish Regalia from Dunnottar Castle—a matter about which there has been considerable dispute. He built-on the large and stately south front and east wing to the old mansion, in the period between then and 1700, which completely altered the aspect of the building. But the old late 16th or early 17th-century house of Caskieben still remains at what is now the back or north side.

This appears to have been a tall fortalice on the Z-plan so popular in Aberdeenshire, the main block lying east and west, with square towers projecting to north-east and south-west, and circular stair-towers rising in the northern re-entrants. The walls, rising to four storeys and a garret, are roughcast, and the roofline appears to have suffered alteration. A great deal of low-level domestic outbuilding to the north has not improved the aspect, nor has the enlargement of windows. A dormer on the east front is dated 1665.

The Johnstons had held the estate for many generations.

KEMNAY HOUSE

The nucleus of this old mansion, standing amongst ancient trees on the southern outskirts of Kemnay village, is a tall L-planned tower-house of probably the early 17th century, the wings of which have been extended, that to the north at an early date. A stair-turret rises above second-floor level in the re-entrant angle; otherwise the building is sturdily plain. The windows of the old part are notably smaller than in the extensions. The roughcast walls are cream-washed, and there is no crowstepping now on the gables.

The original doorway was in the re-entrant, now superseded by a more modern entrance at the other side of the house. A curtain-

wall has enclosed a courtyard at the re-entrant side, traces of which remain. The basement is vaulted, with the old kitchen at the north end of that wing.

Kemnay belonged to the Douglases of Glenbervie in the 16th century, but passed to Sir Thomas Crombie, who is said to have built the present house.

Thomas Burnett, of the Leys family, bought Kemnay in 1688. He long resided at the Court of Hanover and his strong Hanoverianism drew upon him the resentment of local Jacobites. These influenced their French allies, and when the laird was passing through Paris he was arrested and thrown into the Bastille, where he languished until the Duchess of Orleans obtained his release. In the 1790s the Burnett of Kemnay was a noted agriculturalist and tree-planter, and was the first in Aberdeenshire to grow turnips in fields.

KINNAIRD'S HEAD CASTLE

This is a well-known landmark in the town of Fraserburgh, and from the sea, for the castle stands on the very tip of Kinnaird's Head where the Aberdeenshire coastline turns west to flank the Moray Firth. It was, as a consequence, turned into a lighthouse in 1787, by superimposing a lamp on the flat roof within its parapet, an unusual fate for such a fortalice—but one which at least ensures its preservation.

It is a massive oblong tower of simple outline, said to have been built in 1570 by Sir Alexander Fraser of Philorth, but having a more ancient aspect. The theory is that he erected this tower to accommodate himself during his supervision of the construction of the harbour he built at Faithlie in that year, and which was later called Fraserburgh; but this seems altogether improbable, especially as his house of Philorth was a bare two miles away. He may well have used an already existing castle for this purpose. This substantial fortalice, with its six-foot-thick walls, was certainly built for no temporary purposes. The strange adjoining Wine Tower, which is usually given a slightly earlier date, was probably always an outwork of the original castle.

The main keep, rising four storeys to a parapet, has open rounds at all angles, and machicolated projections in the centre of each face at this level. There may originally have been the usual gabled garret storey within the parapet-walk. The masonry is harled and whitewashed and the walls are somewhat rounded at the angles.

The basement is vaulted, as is the Hall on the first floor. The main doorway has been at this level, an early defensive device. The turnpike stair formerly rose in the north-east angle. Inevitably there has been a great deal of internal alteration to adapt the building for its present purpose. The long window on the east front is particularly unsightly.

The Wine Tower, standing somewhat lower on the promontory about 50 yards away, is an unusual building of very rough masonry, now reduced in height to three storeys, all being vaulted. It is reachable only by a difficult path, its door being only a few feet from the edge of the precipice. Immediately beneath is a large cave, known as the Selches Hole, now inaccessible. There is no internal stair, and no communication between basement and first floor. The latter indeed, is only attainable by a trap door from the second floor, which itself is reached by an outside ladder from the ground. Since there is no window in this first-floor chamber, it probably was intended as a hiding-place which would pass unnoticed by strangers. Curiously enough, despite its general uncouth and inconvenient character, the Wine Tower's upper vault has three finely carved heraldic pendants with mottoes, with the Fraser and Royal arms of James the Fifth, which dates the building from at least the first half of the 16th century. An inscription declares: THE GLORY OF THE HONORABLE IS TO FEIR GOD.

[59]

KNOCK CASTLE

This small but sturdily impressive tower stands on a strong site on top of a hillock at the mouth of Glen Muick, in the Dee valley, a mile south-west of Ballater, a ruin but complete to the wallhead. Built of rough coursed rubble it is a simple oblong on plan, with angle-turrets supported on label corbelling at the two southern angles and an interesting gabled watch-chamber corbelled out above the stairhead in the north-west angle. The tower, which has formerly had a courtyard to the north, is four storeys in height, has medium to small windows, shot-holes in the turrets and the watch-chamber, and an empty panel-space on the north front. The doorway is to the north, formerly within the courtyard, and the turnpike stair has risen close by in the north-west angle, projecting a little internally. The basement vaulting has fallen in as have all other floors. The Hall was on the first floor and had a small private stair in the walling down to the kitchen in the basement.

The 3rd Earl of Huntly, who fell at Flodden, appointed one of his own sons to command Knock Castle, which was important for its strategic placing. The 4th Earl granted Knock to a brother of the Gordon laird of Abergeldie nearby. The feud between the Gordons and the Forbeses raged with increasing bitterness after the Gordon defeat at Corrichie by Mary Queen of Scots' forces,

in 1564. Henry Gordon, second of Knock, was killed in a raid by a company of Forbes and Clan Chattan. He was succeeded by his brother Alexander, who is said to have built the castle as it now stands, at the beginning of the 17th century. It did not long remain unmolested. According to tradition the Forbeses surprised, attacked and slew all his seven sons as they were digging peats nearby. On hearing this dire news, the laird was so overcome that he fell down his own stairway in Knock and was killed also. Forbes of Strathgirnock was summarily condemned and executed for leading this affray, by Gordon of Abergeldie as deputy for Huntly, in his own house, and his lands annexed to Abergeldie— a proceeding sadly typical of the times.

KNOCKHALL CASTLE

This tall old and plain fortalice stands on high ground overlooking the estuary of the Ythan about four miles south-east of Ellon, a landmark for miles around. Although ruinous, it is more or less complete to the wallhead, and interesting in a number of respects, being a late 16th-century house enlarged and altered a century later. The plan is unusual, an L with a square stair-tower projecting, not in the re-entrant as is usual, but midway along the opposite or north front. The rubble walls have dressed quoins, there are a number of early-type wide splayed gunloops, and the chimney copings and window-mouldings are good. The doorway in the re-entrant angle, the door of which has been secured by the usual sliding timber bar in its socket, has a lintel dated 1565, and above are two empty panel spaces. Higher, at third-floor level, is a curious projecting stone shelf, supported by corbelling. This is positioned as would be a machicolation for the defence of the doorway, but there is no sign of an access to it, so that it appears to have been no more than a drip-stone to throw off water from the entrance beneath. The house has had a courtyard to the south, traces of the curtain-walling remaining. A round flanking tower survives to the south-east, with a vaulted basement with shot-holes, its upper storey a doocot.

The basement of the house is unusual in that it contains a vaulted kitchen in the foot of the wing, with the normal wide fireplace, sink and drain; and at the same time, in the foot of the main block another and larger vaulted apartment, also provided with sink and drain but no fireplace. Possibly this was a well-chamber. It has a hatch in the vault to the Hall on the first floor.

[61]

The upper floors are now inaccessible, but appear to have been well supplied with garderobes.

Knockhall was built by Henry, 3rd Lord Sinclair of Newburgh in 1565, a great supporter of the Reformation, but sold in 1633 to a son of Udny of that Ilk. In 1693 it was attacked and captured by a Covenant party under the Earl of Erroll and the Earl Marischal, the laird belonging to the other faction. The following year a foraging group from Aberdeen assailed the place, which was not defended by the Lady Udny, her husband being absent. In 1734 the house was accidentally burned and has since remained in a state of ruin.

LEITH HALL

This is a most unusual house of much attractiveness and character situated in a large estate in upper Strathbogie, a mile north of Kennethmont. Now consisting of four wings grouped around a wholly enclosed courtyard reached only by a pend through that to the west, the original house, built in 1650, can be identified fairly readily as the north wing—although the south wing was constructed in accurate imitation thereof at the end of the 18th century, even to the provision of angle-turrets. The west and east wings, with the small round towers, are of mainly mid-18th-century building.

The original house has been a simple rectangular block of three storeys and an attic, with angle-turrets at all four corners and

dormer windows—rather after the style of Monboddo House, Kincardineshire, but taller. The walls are roughcast and yellow-washed, the old windows comparatively small, and the gables are not crowstepped. The entrance was to the south, now within the courtyard, the doorway being surmounted by the arms of James Leith, the builder, now much weather-worn.

Internally, the basement is vaulted, and would contain the original kitchen, with the Hall on first floor and bedroom accommodation above. There has been, of course, much alteration to meet later requirements and additions.

The Leith family were landowners in Aberdeenshire from the 13th century onwards. holding numerous properties including Leslie and Edingarioch in the adjoining parish. In 1650, James Leith, formerly of New Leslie, and thirteenth in descent from William Leith of Barns, Provost of Aberdeen in 1350, built Leith Hall on the property then called Peilside, allegedly on the site of an earlier fortalice known as Peill Castle. His descendants produced many eminent soldiers. One, General Alexander, raised the Royal Aberdeenshire Regiment and was distinguished for his part in the Napoleonic Wars. He succeeded his great-uncle, Andrew Hay of Rannes, a noted Jacobite, in that estate also, and took the name of Leith-Hay, dying in 1838. His son, Sir Andrew Leith-Hay M.P., was also an author and artist, and his book on some of the castellated residences of Aberdeenshire is famous. The last of the direct line, Charles, was killed in the late war aged twenty-one. In 1945 Mrs Leith-Hay of Rannes presented Leith Hall to the National Trust for Scotland. Members of the family still reside there, however.

LESLIE CASTLE

Standing close to the village of Leslie, three miles south-west of Insch, this large and well-planned house, though now ruinous, is especially interesting as illustrating the late date at which defensive fortalices were being built in the North-East. The present building is dated 1661, but many of its features are more typical of a century earlier. The house, which stood within a courtyard, with a surrounding moat, drawbridge and gatehouse, belongs to the L-plan, with a square stair-tower rising in the re-entrant. There are three storeys and an attic, the stair-tower reaching a storey higher, and circular turrets grace each main angle. The gables are not crowstepped and the chimneys are unusual, placed diagonally in Tudor fashion. The windows are fairly large and numerous, and there are many gunloops and shot-holes.

The entrance is in the foot of the stair-tower, surmounted by a weatherworn lintel. Nearby is a stone inscribed FUNDED JUN 17 1661. The Forbes arms are displayed in various positions. The basement is vaulted and in the main block contains the kitchen with great fireplace in the west gable and a stone trough for water supply. There are two vaulted cellars in the wing to the east, one, the wine-cellar, with the usual private stair to the Hall above. The

[64]

main stairway is wide and squared. The first floor main block contains the Hall and withdrawing-room, with a large fireplace having a heraldic lintel. The private room in the wing at this level has an unusual vaulted strongroom in the north-east angle. It has also had an outer door for reaching the garden by means of a removable timber stair. There has been ample bedroom accommodation higher.

Bertolf, a Fleming, acquired the lands of Lesselyn, in the Garioch in the 12th century, and his descendants took the name of Leslie. The last of this line married, at the beginning of the 17th century, a daughter of Patrick, Lord Lindores, son of the 4th Earl of Rothes, of another branch of the Leslie family. She survived her husband and then married John Forbes, son of Monymusk. By redeeming the debts on the Leslie estate he became the possessor of the barony. His son, William Forbes of Leslie rebuilt the castle and died in 1670, *his* son John thereafter selling it to the Leiths of Leith Hall.

LICKLEYHEAD CASTLE

Situated on the bank of the Gadie, three miles south of Insch and two east of Leslie Castle, Lickleyhead is a tall and handsome 17th-century house, modernised and added to but with its ancient character well retained. It follows a modification of the favoured L-plan, with a main block lying east and west, having two-storeyed circular turrets at its northern angles, and with a wing projecting southwards so as to provide two re-entrant angles. In the western of these rises a long and narrow stair-turret corbelled out to the square at top to give access to a watch-chamber in the gabled top storey of the wing. The roughcast walls rise to three storeys, an attic and a garret, the gables are crowstepped, and the dormer windows have decorative pediments. The upper windows of the angle-turrets are circular, as at Castle Fraser.

The entrance is in the main re-entrant to the south, and is dated 1629. The basement is vaulted, containing kitchen and cellar with small slit windows. A good wide turnpike stair rises to the first floor, above which the ascent is continued by the turret stair. The Hall is an excellent apartment of much character. Indeed the entire interior has been lovingly restored by the present proprietrix and makes a most attractive home.

Although Lickleyhead is assumed to date from 1629, it may well contain an older nucleus, for it was discovered during renovations

that the fireplace of the Hall had been rebuilt seven times, the earliest being of 16th-century type. Certainly there was a Patrick Leith of Lickleyhead in 1574, son of the Laird of Edingarioch, descended from Leith of Barns, the ancestor of the Leith Hall family. Another Patrick Leith sold Lickleyhead in 1625 to William Forbes, fiar of Leslie nearby—who presumably built the house as it now appears. The Forbeses held Lickleyhead until the end of the 17th century, whereafter it passed to Hays, Duffs, Gordons and others. The house was occupied in 1645 by William Forbes, natural son of John Forbes of Leslie, who shot off his own hand whilst firing a gun, an accident considered by Spalding to be a judgement for the shooting of Alexander Irvine of Kincausie at the Craibstone in 1644. Forbes had been seeking to earn the reward of 5,000 merks offered by the Covenanting authorities for the capture of Irvine, accused of being a Montrose supporter. Though at the time considered to have rendered the faithful an excellent service by this killing, after the Restoration Forbes was arrested and executed for the murder.

LOGIE-ELPHINSTONE

This is one of those two-faced houses, presenting to the world very different aspects, depending upon the side from which it is viewed. From north and west it is a plain, substantial, late-style mansion of no great character; but from east and south it shows a picturesque 17th-century frontage, within a courtyard. It stands on the Urie, at 'the back of Benachie' three miles east of Oyne and quite close to the other fortalices of Westhall, Pitcaple, Harthill and Pittodrie.

The building has been so altered internally as well as externally, as to leave few of the original features evident. But the nucleus has been a tall old house, dating probably from the early 17th century, of three storeys and a garret, the walls roughcast, oblong on plan with a still taller stair-tower rising at the north-east angle. Later subsidiary buildings project eastwards to form three sides of a courtyard, which is enclosed by a curtain-wall pierced by an arched gateway surmounted by heraldic devices. Further armorial stones, possibly from former dormer pediments, have been inserted in a single storey extension which masks the basement of the main block to the east.

Between 1670 and 1677 James Elphinstone had charters of Logie. He was son and heir of Elphinstone of Ressiviot, of the Glack family, and was created a baronet in 1701. He made additions to the house. His arms, impaling Denholm of West Shield in Lanarkshire, those of his wife, are amongst the collection of panels. He also purchased the fortalice of Craighouse, in Edinburgh. In 1754 Mary, heiress of Sir James Elphinstone, carried the property to her husband, Colonel Robert Dalrymple, of the

[67]

North Berwick family. It is recorded that the famous attainted Lord Pitsligo, so long in hiding after the Forty-five, used frequently to be a secret guest at Logie House of an evening, when in hiding on Benachie, the lady of the house complaining that too much hard drinking went on between the gallant Colonel and the unfortunate Jacobite peer—who of course had the chill mists of Benachie to warm out of his bones. The son of this match took the name of Dalrymple-Horne-Elphinstone, his father having inherited the Horne property of Westhall adjoining. The baronetcy was renewed for this son, and still survives, although the family sold Logie in 1903.

MIDMAR CASTLE

Midmar is one of the finest and most attractive of all the attractive tower-houses of the North-East, and it is sad that today it stands empty in an aspect of neglect. It occupies a picturesque site on a terrace above the Gormack Burn on the northern slopes of the Hill of Fare two miles west of Echt.

Belonging probably to the late 16th century, with additions of about a century later, it has belonged to the Z-plan type, of main block with diagonally opposite towers, that to the south-east being circular and to the north-west, square. The main house rises to four storeys and a garret, but the large circular tower to six storeys, whereafter it finishes with a flat roof surrounded by a

crenellated parapet. There are two stair-turrets, one rising above first floor level in the west re-entrant angle, with a conical roof, and another projecting on picturesque corbelling in the opposite re-entrant, from second-floor level, this ending in an ogee-roofed caphouse to give access to the flat roof of the round tower. Ordinary round angle-turrets grace the gable of the square tower to the west, and unusual very shallow square turrets, with gabled roofs, project on label mouldings at the north-east and south-west corners of the main block. The roofs are typically steep and the walls roughcast. The additions to north and east are much lower, with the original house seeming to dwarf them.

Midmar has undergone more than the usual number of changes of ownership, and, curiously enough suffered many changes of name also. A family of Browns held this property from the 13th century until 1422, when it came into the hands of a branch of the great House of Gordon, like so much of Aberdeenshire. But the Gordons did not retain it long, and it was named Ballogie when Alexander Forbes of the Tolquhon family acquired it towards the close of the 17th century. Again no lengthy period elapsed before it changed hands, this time to a member of the family of Grant, who changed the name to Grantfield. Alexander Grant of Grantfield was appointed Sheriff-principal of Aberdeenshire in 1741. By 1782 however it was Midmar again, and in the hands of an heiress, Margaret Davidson, only child of a Provost of Aberdeen. She carried it in marriage to one of the Elphinstones of Logie-Elphinstone, who in turn sold it to his own brother-in-law, James Mansfield, a banker, about 1795. One of his grand-daughters heired Midmar and sold it to a Gordon again, Colonel Gordon of Cluny, in 1842, and it has remained with his descendants. It all seems a somewhat odd and pedestrian story for so noble a fortalice.

It is to be hoped that this attractive and unusual house will be preserved and put to some useful purpose.

HOUSE OF MONYMUSK

In a fine estate and attractive setting on the Don, near Monymusk village, this tall and commodious old house is a structure of various periods. While the lofty and massive central tower is reputed to have been built by Willam Forbes in 1587, there may well be previous monastic work incorporated, the smaller round tower to the south being said to be older.

The main L-planned house is now of five storeys, but the two upper storeys are an 18th-century addition, the corbelling for a parapet still projecting above second-floor level on the east front, and that of angle-turrets at the same level to the west (as seen in sketch). A tiny semi-turret projects in the south-west re-entrant at third-floor level. The later upper works do not enhance the aspect, and lower, more modern buildings have been added to south and east. The walls are roughcast and yellow-washed. Many windows have been enlarged.

William Forbes of Corsindae is said to have siezed the Priory of Monymusk at the Reformation. This family descended from Duncan, second son of the 2nd Lord Forbes. They retained possession until Sir Francis Grant, Lord Cullen of Session, sold Cullen and bought this property in 1712. His son, Sir Alexander, is reputed to have planted more trees than anyone else in Britain, 50 million in fifty years, allowing his son and grandson to sell £20,000 worth of timber—more than their great-grandfather paid for the entire property. The family of Grant of Monymusk is still in possession.

MOUNIE CASTLE

This delightful small fortalice, dating apparently from the early 17th century, stands about three miles west of Oldmeldrum. It conforms to the T-plan, with a long main block of three storeys running north and south, and a circular stair-tower projecting westwards midway along the west front. This is corbelled out to the square at the top to house a watch-chamber, reached by a turret stair in the south-west re-entrant angle. The corbelling here is quite elaborate. The walling is otherwise plain and roughcast, and the gables crowstepped. A more modern detached wing for domestics has been added to the south-west.

The entrance is in the foot of the stair-tower, but two more modern doorways have been opened on either side on this west front. The basement contains two vaulted chambers, that to the south being the kitchen, with a wide arched fireplace and a stone basin nearby. The Hall on the first floor has been subdivided by later partitions, and there have been other alterations at this level; the small turret stair, for instance, is now inaccessible.

Mounie was a possession of the Seton family, cadets of Alexander Seton, the famous Earl of Dunfermline and Chancellor of Scotland in the 17th century. Pitmedden nearby was an important Seton seat, and George Seton of Mounie was second son of Lord Pitmedden. There are many Seton portraits and mementoes in the house, including a picture of John Seton of Aquhorties,

Chamberlain to the Earl of Dunfermline. Mounie passed from
Seton hands for a period, but later returned to that family.

PITCAPLE CASTLE

This fine house stands in its ancient estate on the bank of the River
Urie five miles north-west of Inverurie. Now a good example of
the Z-plan, with the main block lying north and south and round
towers projecting to north-east and south-west, it appears to date
from the early 17th century; but there is older work included. The
walls, rising to three storeys and an attic, are roughcast. An angle-
turret graces the south-east corner, and a tiny stair-turret projects
in the re-entrant between the south-west round tower and the
main south gable. The peculiar shape of the tower and turret roofs
is something of a modernisation, for the castle had fallen into a
bad state of repair and was largely renovated about 1830 when
these roofs were built, the main roof-level altered, and the crowstepping of the gables removed, in an attempt by the then laird to
copy the chateau architecture of France. Recently, when the house
was being re-harled, early 16th-century type gunloops were discovered in the north-east or Thane's tower, with circular shot-
holes elsewhere. The castle was originally surrounded by a moat
and outer curtain-wall, with a gatehouse at its south-western
angle and a drawbridge.

The original entrance was in the foot of the south-west round
tower. The basement of the main block is vaulted, as are four
storeys of the Thane's tower. The Hall, as usual, is on the first
floor, with bedroom accommodation above. One of these chambers, on the second floor, is known as the King's Room. Here
Charles the Second spent a night in July 1650 after having landed
at Garmouth from exile in Holland.

James the Second, in 1457 confirmed a charter of Pitcaple to
David Leslie, son of Sir William Leslie, 4th of Balquhain nearby,
head of a prominent and powerful family. The original castle
probably dates from that period. The Leslies were wild as well as
powerful, and Pitcaple had an eventful history. The 4th laird
killed George Leith of Freefield, and in consequence his family
and the many Leiths of the area became at feud; he was eventually
forced to leave the country, and died a captain in the Emperor's
army. James the Fourth visited here, as did his grand-daughter
Mary Queen of Scots, when in 1562 she made her progress into
the North to demolish the power of the Gordons. She had spent

the night at Balquhain, but curiously enough is said to have break-
fasted here. She is reputed to have planted a thorn tree—under
which her great-grandson Charles danced a century later—and
which survived until 1856. It is now replaced by a red maple,
planted by a later Queen Mary in 1923.

In 1630, James Leslie, second son of the laird, was implicated
in the terrible tragedy of the burning of the House of Frendraught, which set the North of Scotland by the ears for some
time. The laird himself died at the Battle of Worcester in 1651,
fighting for the King he had entertained at Pitcaple—buying up
all the claret in the neighbourhood to do so—the year before.
Here, the same troubled century, the great Montrose was brought
a prisoner on his way to his death at Edinburgh, after having been
betrayed by Macleod of Assynt, preceded by a herald crying,
'Here comes James Graham, a traitor to his country!' The room
where he was lodged is still pointed out, and tradition has it that
the lady of the house would have engineered his escape had the
Marquis agreed.

The Leslies retained possession until 1757 when Sir James died
and his half-sister Jane carried the property to her husband, Pro-
fessor John Lumsden, of King's College. Their daughters sold
Pitcaple to Harry Lumsden of the Cushnie family nearby, with
whose descendants it still remains.

PITFICHIE CASTLE

This ruinous late 16th-century fortalice stands a mile north of Monymusk on the right bank of Don. It consists of a rectangular block of four storeys and a garret, with a large round tower projecting at the south-west angle. A semi-circular stair-turret rises in the eastern re-entrant, corbelled out to the square on a label moulding to end in a gabled caphouse. A square corner turret enhances the north-west angle. Two massive chimney-stacks, curved, are a feature of the round tower. The doorway, in the western re-entrant has been altered in position during construction to enter by the base of the round tower instead of the main block—no doubt for internal security. It gives access to a guard-room, the kitchen, a further cellar, and a communicating passage, all vaulted; also to the stair-foot. The Hall on the first floor and sleeping accommodation above, now inaccessible, followed the usual pattern. The fabric, now in a bad condition, is pierced by various shot-holes.

Pitfichie belonged to the family of Urrie or Hurry, of which came the famed General Hurry of the Civil Wars. In 1650 William Urrie of Pitfichie and others raided tenants' houses of Forbes of Forneidlie, maltreating wives and actually seeking to burn alive babies 'lyand in thair creddillis', driving off cattle to Pitfichie—for which he was duly outlawed. Seven years later Pitfichie passed to the Forbeses of nearby Monymusk. In the Rising of 1715 John Forbes of Pitfichie was a Collector of Cess for the Jacobite army.

PITSLIGO CASTLE

This large and impressive castle, situated half-a-mile east of Rose-hearty in Buchan, is really more ruinous than it is my practice to include in these volumes; but its importance, its many interesting features, and the fact that its plan and growth are still so readily apparent, plead for its inclusion.

The site is the same ridge, half-a-mile back from the rocky coast, as that on which stands the later Fraser castle of Pittullie. The building has developed from a massive simple square keep of the early 15th century, into a major courtyard-type establishment, with a tall flanking drum-tower at the north-east angle and subsidiary buildings completely enclosing a large central court, the whole being surrounded by a pleasance within a high wall, with an arched gateway to the west. Over this gateway is a panel containing the impaled arms of Forbes and Erskine, with the initials of Alexander, 2nd Lord Pitsligo, and Mary Erskine his wife, and the date of his succession, 1663.

The original keep, now only a ruined shell, has been of great strength, with walls nine feet in thickness. There have been two main vaulted storeys, with entresols or half-floors. The parapet and floor above the upper vault has now gone. The flanking stair-tower and attached building at the north-east corner is in better condition however, being complete to the parapet and well defended with wide splayed gunloops. Over its courtyard doorway is a panel containing the royal arms of Scotland with crown and the initials I.R. for King James the Sixth, dated 1577. James was only eleven at this time, and the panel can represent only a gesture in loyalty. On the east wall of the same tower is another royal panel, with crown, quartering the arms of Scotland, England, Ireland and France, and dated 1603, celebrating the Union of the Crowns. The inclusion of the French arms is interesting, indicating the swing away from the sentiment of the Auld Alliance, following on the English succession.

The subsidiary buildings and courtyard, although now in a state of great neglect, indeed given over to pigs, offer still a notable impression of grandeur and strength. This, so close to the centres of Fraserburgh and Rosehearty, is surely a monument which the Ministry of Works ought to take in hand.

Pitsligo was a Fraser property, but came into the hands of Sir William Forbes, son of Sir John Forbes of Druminnor, chief of that great family, by his marriage with the only daughter of Sir William Fraser of Philorth in the first half of the 15th century. In

[75]

1633 Alexander Forbes was created Lord Pitsligo, a title forfeited by his great-grandson, the famous Alexander, for his share in the Rising of 1745. The story of Lord Pitsligo's prolonged wanderings and hidings from the authorities thereafter has become enshrined in Scottish history. His house ought to be enshrined likewise.

PITTODRIE HOUSE

Standing high in a large wooded estate on the north flank of Benachie, a mile west of Chapel of Garioch, Pittodrie is a most difficult house to describe clearly. The ancient nucleus towers picturesquely out of a surrounding mass of building of various periods, but to trace the original lay-out internally poses many problems. Over the doorway of a modern porch is the date 1605, with the Erskine coat-of-arms; this might well be the date of the central mass of the house. Elsewhere the date 1675 may refer to the earliest extensions. But a detached wing to the north contains vaulted cellars, with two gunloops, and appears to belong to a still earlier house.

The early 17th-century house would seem to have followed a variation of the L-plan, forming two re-entrants, in the southern of which rises a truncated stair-tower, square but the stair within it a circular turnpike. Another tall and circular stair-tower, with a conical roof, rises at the north-west angle of one wing (as in sketch). Internally the house has been so greatly altered and modernised, to link up with the many additions, as to make any attempted description valueless. There is no vaulting in this part of the house.

Pittodrie was an Erskine property. The founder of the line was Sir Thomas Erskine of Halton, second son of the John Erskine of Dun who fell at Flodden. In 1525 he became Secretary to the youthful James the Fifth, and retained the appointment until the King's death in 1542. He was knighted and made Warden of the rebellious Angus's castle of Tantallon, marrying Elizabeth, daughter of Sir James Scrymgeour of Dudhope. He had a charter of Pittodrie in 1558. In 1635, John, Earl of Mar, himself an Erskine, issued a commission to John Erskine of Pittodrie, and others, to be his bailies in Mar. The sixth descendant was an heiress, Mary Erskine, who married Colonel Henry Knight, who took the name of Erskine, and the property continued for some generations with their descendants.

PITTULIE CASTLE

Interesting and unusual, this fairly late castle occupies an open position on rising ground above the sea a mile east of Rosehearty, and only half-a-mile from the larger castle of Pitsligo, both properties having belonged to the Frasers of Philorth. Pittulie appears to date from the very end of the 16th century, and consists of a long and comparatively low main block, with a taller square tower at the north-west corner, the stair-turret for which now projects high above all in unusual fashion. Other highly unusual features

are the low placing of the angle-turrets which crown the south-east and south-west gables, the corbelling for which is only a dozen feet above the ground; and the unique squared turret-like windows projecting on the northern angles of the tower. The main block is only two storeys and an attic in height. The main stair rises in the square tower to first-floor level only, and a secondary turret-stair is corbelled out thereafter, from the Hall at that level, on the north front. The earlier-mentioned higher stair-turret rises from second-floor level to give access to the upper floors of the tower. The building is now very ruinous, the masonry being a rough grey rubble with good ashlar dressings and decorative work. High on the north face of the tower, between the elaborate cornerwise windows is a diamond-shaped aperture, further to lighten the already well-lit 'laird's-room'.

The original entrance, within a cable moulding, is in the north front of the tower also, and is surmounted by a double empty panel-space under a tympanum. The basement of the house is not vaulted, and contained kitchen and cellarage. The very large Hall on the first floor had a fireplace at each end, with a private mural stair down to the wine-cellar. There is a smaller room off. A square shot-hole opens off a wall-cupboard on the south front.

Although the date 1651 appears on a skew-putt of the east gable, the house probably was built at least fifty years earlier. The lands were held by the Frasers from the 14th century, and in 1596 Alexander Fraser of Fraserburgh granted Over and Nether Pittulie to his son also Alexander, on his marriage to Margaret Abernethy of Saltoun. It was probably for this couple that the castle was erected. The husband subscribed his will 'at Pittullie' in July 1650, so the house certainly pre-dates the skew-putt. As a result of this marriage, the Frasers inherited the Saltoun peerage, which they still hold, Lord Saltoun living at nearby Cairnbulg Castle, although Pittulie later passed to the Cumine family. The castle is said to have been inhabited until 1850.

HOUSE OF SHIVAS

The fine House of Shivas stands in rolling country in the Ythan valley about three miles east of Methlick, in the parish of Tarves. It is a tall L-planned fortalice apparently of the late 16th century, which was all but gutted by fire in 1900, and which has been both 'restored' and 'de-restored' since, and now stands within a courtyard—which no doubt it did originally—but which is modern. The plan varies from the normal L in that the wing is off-set somewhat to the west to give added protective cover to that front; also a wide circular stair-tower projects on the inner or north front of the main block. A stair-turret rises within the main re-entrant angle. Lower additions now extend both wings.

The entrance from the courtyard is in the re-entrant and is notable for the elaborate and interesting arrangement of its protective shot-holes. There are four groups, circular and diamond-shaped, at various points around the doorway, very similar to those at Tolquhon Castle in the same parish. An empty panel-space surmounts the entrance, which is still provided with its draw-bar in deep recess in the masonry.

The basement is vaulted, containing the kitchen to the east and two cellars, reached by a vaulted passage. The foot of the wing is occupied by a squared stair now of timber, giving access to the first floor only, above which the ascent is continued by the narrow turret stair in the re-entrant. The wider turnpike in the round tower serves all floors. The Hall is a fine panelled apartment, 26 by 17 feet, with large fireplace, garderobe and aumbries; also a recess with the sacred monogram i.h.s. and a cross. A private room opens to the east. The second floor has contained, as well as two bedrooms, an Upper Hall, now subdivided. There is the usual attic accommodation above, and an extra or mezzanine floor is contrived in the wing.

There is a well in the courtyard, long covered over but now restored. The famous Mary Gray Tree, a plane, grows nearby.

The family of Shivas of that Ilk seem to have failed at an early date, although no doubt the notorious Archbishop Schevez, astrologer and James Third's Primate of St. Andrews, was a descendant. Heiresses carried the property to Lipps and Mait-

lands. George, Lord Gordon gained Shivas in 1467, but by 1509 there is mention of Thomas Gray of Scheves—though the Gordons seem to have maintained some sort of superiority, for Sir George Gordon of Schives is mentioned frequently between 1530 and 1568. However, by the end of the 16th century the Grays were established as lairds, and it was probably by them that the present house was built. They were a well-known Catholic family, and the sacred monogram in the Hall no doubt indicates the situation of their private altar. By 1721 Shivas had passed to the powerful local Forbes family, but afterwards reverted to the Gordon Earls of Aberdeen. It is now the delightful residence of Lord Catto.

TERPERSIE CASTLE

This is a ruinous fortalice of the late 16th century, of moderate size but considerable character, set snugly in its own little valley amongst the Correen Hills a mile or so north-west of Tullynestle. It was also known formerly as Dalpersie. A Gordon house, it follows the Z-plan, of a main block lying north and south, with round towers projecting at opposite angles, to north-east and south-west. The walls, of rough coursed rubble, rise to three storeys and a garret and are notably well supplied with shot-holes, so sited as to command every wall-face and approach. A stair-turret is corbelled out in the eastern re-entrant between main block and south tower, above first-floor level. On the bottom corbel of this is the letter G. and on an adjoining window sill a panel dated 1561. The round towers formerly had conical roofs. Unfortunately the entire roofless fabric standing in a farm-steading, is now in a bad condition.

The entrance is in the east front of the main block, and admits directly in the main basement apartment, which would be the kitchen. There are small octagonally vaulted chambers in the foot of each tower. A straight stair within the walling of the south gable rises to the first floor, above which the ascent is by the turret stair. The access to this main stair is from the south round tower, and it is noteworthy that as well as the main door, there are other stout doors, at the tower and the stair-foot, for any intruder to negotiate before he could climb to the laird's living quarters. There has been a 17th century addition to the east containing a wider turnpike stair. The Hall on the first floor has had two good windows, and there have been private small rooms in the towers at this level and above.

William Gordon, the builder, was fourth son of Gordon of Lesmoir. He was a very tough character, present with his chief, Huntly, at the disastrous Battle of Corrichie, Mary Queen of Scots' only victory; ten years later at the Battle of Tillyangus, he was largely responsible for victory by killing Black Arthur Forbes, brother of Lord Forbes and champion of that clan. He was with Adam Gordon of Auchindoun also at the Battle of the Craibstone, and again at the Bourd of Brechin, now fighting on Queen Mary's side. After the Battle of Auldearn in 1645 General Baillie's troops burned Terpersie, A later laird fought at Culloden and after the defeat lurked amongst his own hills for long without detection; at length, one wild night he sought the comfort of his

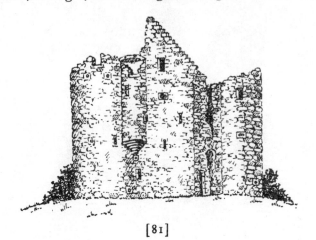

own fireside, and was betrayed to a party of King George's troops, who discovered him hidden in a recess under the roof. There was some doubt as to identity however, until the troops took him to another house where were lodging his wife and children. The latter, seeing him and running to him with shouts of 'Daddy!' unwittingly consigned their parent to the block. He is said to have been the last person executed for a share in the Rising of 1745.

TILLYCAIRN CASTLE

The ruined castle of Tillycairn stands on high ground four miles south-west of Monymusk, beside the modern farm-steading. Not in a good state of repair, it has been a handsome fortalice on the L-plan, with certain refinements. The walls are massive, the lower courses being constructed of great unhewn boulders. The angles are rounded, and a semi-circular stair-tower rises in the re-entrant, its top storey being of dressed stone. Angle-turrets crown the gables, supported on elaborate corbelling, save for that at the south-east which is more plain. There has been a short parapet and walk on the west side of the wing, between the round stair-tower and the south-west turret, an unusual feature. There are numerous gunloops, some provided with cross-shaped slits above for improved aiming.

The basement contains three vaulted chambers, one being the kitchen with its wide arched fireplace. The Hall occupies all the main block first floor, having a fine fireplace, a stone sink and drain, and also a laird's lug, or listening device, leading to a closet above the fireplace. The private room in the wing has a fireplace and an aumbry. There was bedroom accommodation above.

Tillycairn looks a strong and warlike place, but the only historical reference I have found to it is peaceable and literary. It was the fortalice of Matthew Lumsden, who died in 1580, brother of the Laird of Cushnie, and author of the well-known work, *The Genealogical History of the House of Forbes*. It has been a fine house of its period.

PLACE OF TILLYFOUR

Picturesquely situated on the east bank of the River Don, where it winds through the Benachie range in a narrow wooded defile, five miles north-west of Monymusk, the old Place of Tillyfour is an interesting small fortalice of the 16th century which eventually fell on evil days, sank into neglect, and was drastically restored and added to in 1884. The restoration was ably done, in a copy of the early style, so that at first or even second glance, where original work merges into modern is not always easy to trace. Also there has been much earlier alteration, probably in the first half of the 17th century, and the roof-level has been changed, so that a reconstruction of the original house is made the more difficult. It seems, however, that the first fortalice was a most sturdy, almost squat, house of two storeys and a garret, on a variation of the L-plan, whereby the two wings join in such a way as to produce a re-entrant angle at both sides, in the eastern of which a short stair-turret is corbelled out from first-floor level, supported on a squinch—one of the comparatively few examples of this architectural device in Aberdeenshire, another being at nearby Westhall. A courtyard lies to the south, entered by an arched gateway.

The door is in the western re-entrant and over it is a renewed panel bearing the date 1626. It is still protected by a massive draw-bar in its deep socket within the thickness of the walling. A porter's apartment adjoins, and there are a number of slit windows. Internally the house has been almost entirely gutted, and no vaulting remains, but the kitchen appears to have been in the west wing basement. The fairly massive chimney-stack at the western gable may represent an early addition, where a somewhat

narrower extension has been built on to this wing. This extension is said to have contained a draw-well, now filled in.

The house is in excellent condition and highly attractive.

Originally Tillyfour belonged to the Earldom of Mar, as part of the Lordship of Garioch, and the Place was used as a hunting-seat. By an Assize of Error the lands were forfeited to the Crown in the 15th century, and bestowed by James the Fourth on Sir John Leslie of Wardhouse, of the Balquhain family, in 1508, with the office of Bailie of the Crown lands in the Garioch. It seems probable that this laird built the oldest part of the present house, although there must have been earlier work on the site. He was married five times and died in 1546. His grandson, dying 1602, was Falconer to James the Sixth. *His* grandson, Sir John, was created a baronet of Nova Scotia in 1628. He married Elizabeth Gordon of Newton, and allegedly by her infidelities and his own extravagance and dissipation, lost much of his lands. There may have been malice in this theory, however, for we read that they were 'contumacious Papists' and that in 1638 the Bishop of Aberdeen was excommunicated by the Assembly, amongst the crimes imputed to him being that 'at the request of Elizabeth Gordon, Lady Wardhouse, ane infamous woman, he consecrated a chapell at Tillyfour after a superstitious forme and manner.' Sir John died in 1640 and 'was buriet within his awen chapell at Tullifour quhair never laird of Wardes was buriet befoire'. The chapel stood in a corner of the courtyard. His widow was married to Sir Alexander Gordon of Cluny within six months of his death, and the lands passed from the Leslies.

TOLQUHON CASTLE

This handsome fortalice, long the seat of a powerful branch of the Forbes family, though ruinous, is now in the care of the Ministry of Works. It lies, some distance from a main road, two miles south of Tarves, and with its splendid drum-towered gatehouse and inner and outer courts makes a most impressive picture.

The original building was a simple rectangular 15th-century tower, erected by the Prestons of Craigmillar in Lothian. This now forms the north-east angle of the courtyard. The remainder, better preserved, was completed in 1587, and fills up the other three sides, including the excellent gatehouse range. The major work lies to the south and comprises a three-storeyed main block, with a circular stair-tower, corbelled out to the square at the top, projecting centrally into the courtyard; also a square gabled tower at each end—that to the east thrusting out beyond the overall rectangle in a salient. Lower, subsidiary wings extend to east and west, and to balance the south-east tower, another, circular on plan, thrusts out at the north-west angle. Thus is formed a more elaborate plan than usual, comprising two Zs rather than two Ls.

The building standards are high throughout. The courtyard windows are large for the period, there are stringcourses, label-mouldings and heraldic decorations, and a liberal supply of gun-loops and triple shot-holes.

The very ruinous Preston Tower has been a typical thick-walled, vaulted and parapeted keep. The remainder of the building is mainly complete to the wallhead however. The entrance is by an arched doorway from the court, in the foot of the south-west square tower, giving access to a long vaulted passage in the main block from which are reached three vaulted cellars, and also the kitchen at the far east end. This has the usual large fireplace, stone sink, and hatch. Both it and the wine-cellar at the west have private stairs to the Hall and laird's room above. Beyond the kitchen, in the south-east tower, was the bakehouse and ovens, at basement level. Also at this level, although reached only by a trap-door from above, was the unpleasant L-shaped pit or prison.

The first floor was reached by a wide curved stair in the south-west tower, with guardroom at foot. The Hall has a large moulded fireplace and a floor of hexagonal flagstones. Off it to the east is the laird's private room, with a tiny oratory in the south-east corner. A secret chamber adjoins, reached from a trap-door above. A turnpike stair in the central round tower gives access to bedrooms higher.

The lower ranges flanking the courtyard are less substantial and more ruinous. That to the west contained a long gallery, with cellars beneath. Opening from the gallery, the north-west circular tower has a vaulted bedroom at this level, and a turret stair leading to another bedroom above.

The gatehouse range to the north is extremely picturesque, with its twin drum towers and arched pend between, flanked by triple shot-holes, armorial carvings and moulded stringcourses. The Forbes arms are surmounted by the escutcheon of James the Sixth, and to the right is a finely wrought panel inscribed AL THIS WARKE. EXCEP THE AULD TOUR. WAS BEGVN BE WILLIAM FORBES 15 APRILE. 1584. AND ENDIT BE HIM. 20 OCTOBER 1589. The original iron yetts here are a notable feature.

The Forbeses acquired Tolquhon by the marriage of Sir John, brother of the first Lord Forbes, with the Preston heiress in 1420. The builder of the 16th-century extensions entertained King Jamie Saxt here soon after its completion, in 1589, during the royal campaign to crush the rebellion of Huntly and the Catholic earls. The Gordons, of course, were ever enemies of Forbes. He had, in 1582, been granted a curious exemption from military service because of 'ane dolour and diseaiss in his ene, proceiding be ane distellatioun out of the heid' whereby he was permitted 'to eit flesche with thre or foure with him in companie in the forbidden tyme' (Lent). His predecessor fell at the Battle of Pinkie, and the tenth laird saved Charles Second's life at the Battle of Worcester in 1651, and was knighted. The Forbes tenure of Tolquhon ended in 1716.

TOWIE BARCLAY CASTLE

It would be a great mistake to omit this most interesting castle from this compendium, even although its present appearance is so altered as to bear little resemblance to its original state—one of the normal conditions I make for inclusion. Towie Barclay is a special case, even if its two upper storeys, with parapet and rounds were shorn off in 1792, the present roofline therefore being as false as it is out-of-proportion. The remaining work, however, especially the interior, merits description.

Towie Barclay, not to be confused with the fragmentary Towie Castle in Strathdon, stands in the Ythan valley four miles south of Turriff, quite close to the main highway. As well as the wrong impression given by its appearance, the building has been be-devilled by an undue reputation for extreme antiquity, it frequently being claimed to belong to the 12th century. This is because of an inscribed panel on the south front declaring: SIR ALEXANDER OF TOLLY FOUNDATOR DECEISIT ANNO DOMINI 1136. On the same stone however, is carved also: IN TIM OF VALTH AL MEN SEMIS FRINDLY AND FRINDIS NOT KNAUIN BUT IN ADVERSITY 1593. Clearly the earlier part of the inscription is merely a record of a previous building. Nevertheless, the original work that remains appears to date from somewhat earlier than 1593.

The L-plan is of unusual proportions. The red sandstone walls rise, above a plinth, only three storeys to the modern parapet and flat roof, and there are wide squared gunloops at basement level. The main block lies north and south, with the wing projecting eastwards, and in the re-entrant angle are two doorways, that in the wing, obviously of later date, inscribed I.G. and E.B. 1604. The earlier, and original doorway had a defaced panel above, with scroll.

The basement contains three vaulted chambers, entered from a most elaborately groined vaulted vestibule. There is an L-shaped guardroom to the right, the entrance being defended by an in-geniously designed gunloop from which it is possible to fire in two directions whilst the defender himself is protected by a stone pillar to deflect missiles from without. A good wide stair, reached from a long vaulted passage, rises in the wing, while a smaller service stair connects with the Hall, in the south-west angle.

This Hall is a magnificent apartment, 30 by 20 feet, with a fine ribbed and groined vault in two sections, springing from carved corbels. There is a 10-feet wide fireplace with stone seats and aumbries, and also stone seats in the window embrasures, from

the eastern of which opens a small vaulted chamber. In the south
wall a most elaborate and ornate vaulted gallery opens, like a
minstrels' gallery but probably an oratory, because of the sacred
carvings. It is reached by a small straight stair in the thickness of
the walling. Above has been altered or removed.

The Barclays of Towie were a famous family flourishing here
for 600 years and taking major part in the affairs of Aberdeenshire
and frequently on the wider national stage. Patrick Barclay, whose
rueful reflections of friendship I quoted above, was laird from
1558 to 1624, and suffered much in the cause of Mary Queen of
Scots. The most celebrated of the line was the famous Russian
Army general of the Napoleonic Wars, Prince Michael Barclay
de Tolly.

UDNY CASTLE

This massive fortalice stands within a large estate about four miles
south of Tarves, and although it has had a modern mansion
attached, this has now been demolished and only the old work
remains. Just how old this work may be is a matter for conjecture.
There are two schools of thought. First the more obvious one,
which the external aspect of the building suggests, that the three
lower storeys represent an early thick-walled keep of possibly the
first half of the 15th century, which was heightened probably in
the 16th century and completed with the angle-turrets and present
gables in the early 17th century. To some extent tradition bears

[88]

this out, for legend has it that Udny was built by three lairds, and is said to have ruined them all. MacGibbon & Ross however, consider that the work is in fact more or less homogeneous, all dating from the late 16th or early 17th century. Much as I respect these renowned experts, I must say that the first theory seems to me more likely. The great thickness of the walling, studded with mural chambers, the vaulting on two floors, the small size of the lesser windows, and the fact that there is an evident intake in the masonry above second-floor level, all seem to indicate an early period of construction. Moreover the two great and wide gunloops flanking the door are of an early type.

The first recorded mention of the property seems to have been when Ronald of Uldney had a charter of the lands from David the Second, although it seems improbable that any portion of the present five-storey castle dates from that period. The upper storeys are curious, in that they seem to combine two styles. The open parapet on elaborate corbelling surmounts one wallhead only, which is very unusual. Also the angle-turrets are set notably high in relation to the roofline, and look like an afterthought. They give the impression of open rounds which have been heightened and roofed over; yet their corbelling actually springs from a higher base than that of the parapet, which seems to counter the open round suggestion. The large windows are indeed very large for an early construction.

Whatever the structural truth of the matter, Udny is a tall stronghold, somewhat clumsy-seeming but impressive, rectangular on plan, its harled walls rounded at the angles and provided with ample gunloops and shot-holes.

The arched entrance is in the east front and admits through eight feet of masonry to the small vaulted kitchen and wine-cellar. To the left a newel-stair rises admittedly very wide for an early date. The first floor contains the great Hall, with a vault 20 feet high. The windows here have stone seats, there are mural chambers and a passage in the thickness of the wall to a small bedchamber—all early features. A turnpike stair ascends from a corner of the Hall, over the doorway to which is the legend: LET NO ONE BEAR BEFORE THIS THRESHOLD HENCE, WORDS UTTERED HERE IN FRIENDLY CONFIDENCE. The second floor now contains one chamber, but may have been subdivided once, since the two stairways give access at either end. Above is sleeping accommodation.

The Udnys of that Ilk occupied the property down to recent times. In Mary Queen of Scots' time the laird subscribed to raise forces against the English invaders, and a successor supported

the King against the Covenant. In 1634 John Udny of Udny acquired property in the Belhelvie area and went to live in Knockhall Castle there. Alexander the 12th of his line has become famous because of his employment of James Fleeman (or Fleming) the renowned 'Laird of Udny's Fool', a sort of licenced jester who was instrumental in saving the family from being burned to death in a fire at Knockhall in 1734.

WESTHALL

This small but most attractive fortalice, seemingly of the 16th century, stands on rising ground half-a-mile north of Oyne, with a more modern mansion attached. It appears to date from two early periods. There is an L-shaped parapeted tower of three storeys and a garret, and this has been extended to north and east, probably in the 17th century, by a gabled block with a circular tower at the south-east angle. A stair-turret projects above a squinch, on elaborate label-moulded corbelling in the re-entrant, and the same type of corbelling supports the high crenellated parapet, which has open rounds at the angles. The walls are massive and roughcast, and the original windows small.

The basement is vaulted, and the usual arrangement of Hall on first floor and sleeping accommodation above would apply.

Westhall belonged to the diocese of Aberdeen. At the Reformation the lands appear to have come to a branch of the Gordon family, for there is a Walter Gordon of Westhall in 1589, and James Gordon thereof was Collector of Cess in 1649. In 1681 the Reverend James Horne, Vicar of Elgin, bought the property, after demitting his charge on refusing to subscribe to the Test Act. He married a daughter of the 7th Laird of Pitcaple. His son John, an advocate and a Jacobite, succeeded. He had the lands, with others, erected into the barony of Horne, with its burgh, Old Rayne. Descendants in the female line carried the property to the Dalrymple-Horne-Elphinstone family.

ANGUS

AFFLECK OR AUCHENLECK CASTLE

In Affleck we have an excellent example of a substantial free-standing tower-house of the late 15th century, in a good state of preservation and which has been very little altered. It stands on high ground about a mile west of the parish church of Monikie, and though five miles from the sea, in the past is said to have provided a useful landmark for sailors.

It is a tall tower of five storeys, sixty feet high, oblong on plan save for a tiny projecting wing at the south-east angle to house the turnpike stair. The walling, of good coursed rubble, is sufficiently thick to house a number of mural chambers at various levels. The parapet surrounding the garret storey, which appears to have been rebuilt at some period, has open rounds at all angles, for defence, and has two machicolated projections for the hurling of missiles, boiling pitch or other liquid, one on the east, directly above the doorway, the other on the west. The parapet-walk is unusual in having two caphouses or watch-turrets, of square design, one covering the stairhead, which is usual, the other at the south-west angle. I do not recollect having seen this duplication elsewhere.

Internally the planning is typically simple, but of good workmanship. The basement is subdivided but on each other floor there is only one apartment. The first floor has a vaulted ceiling, supporting the stone floor of the Hall above, which in this instance is on the second floor, another unusual feature. This Hall is a handsome apartment with a fine pillared stone fireplace, windows with stone seats, and wall-closets. In the thickness of the east wall, a tiny staircase of eleven steps, only 33 inches wide, leads up to an equally tiny chamber in the projecting stair-wing, little more than seven feet square. From this very private sanctum a spy-hole looks down into the Hall—no doubt for the use of

the laird or his lady, and a not altogether unusual convenience.

Opening off the floor above is an excellent small oratory, vaulted and provided with holy-water stoup, piscina and aumbry, with decorative corbels for holding candles at either side of the altar—all only seven feet square.

The Auchenlecks of that Ilk are said to have possessed this property from the earliest times. They were hereditary armour-bearers to the Earls of Crawford and one did homage to Edward of England in 1306. By the early 18th century Affleck was owned by a family named Reid. One of this line was forfeited for his share in the ill-fated Rising of 1745, and there is a story of his lady and a serving-maid, seeing government officers coming to take possession, secreting plate of considerable value about their persons and escaping with it to Dundee, *en route* to join the laird in France. A more modern house was built by the new owners.

AIRLIE CASTLE

This famous fortalice, the 'Bonnie Hoose o' Airlie' stands on an exceedingly strong site on a high narrow promontory of rock, fully 100 feet above the junction of the rushing streams of Isla and Melgam, five miles north-east of Alyth. The present impressive buildings date from three periods; the massive and lengthy portion of curtain-wall and part of the northern tower of the original 15th-century fortalice; the gate-tower, altered in the late

16th or early 17th century; and a more modern house behind this front, stretching north-westwards. All that can be seen from the approach (and in the sketch) belongs to the first and second periods.

The original castle of Airlie, or Errolly as it was formerly called, was of great strength, in structure and defensive features as in site. In 1432 Sir Walter Ogilvy of Lintrathen, descended from the first Thane of Angus, received a licence from James First to erect his Tower of Eroly in the form of a castle, and in 1458 Sir John, presumably his son, had a grant of the castle and barony. The building then erected was almost a fortress. A deep ditch, traces of which can still be seen, cut off the apex of the high rocky site above the Den of Airlie, and behind this ditch was built the high and massive curtain-wall (seen more or less intact to the left of the sketch), 120 feet long, 10 feet thick and about 30 feet high, with only two slit-like windows piercing it—these however being splayed out to almost seven feet wide on the inner side. In the centre of this east front rises the gate-tower with its strongly guarded arched gateway, fitted for a portcullis and a second inner door, no doubt of iron grille-work; there would almost certainly be a drawbridge over the ditch also. At the top of the entrance arch is a flue for the pouring down of missiles or boiling liquid on intruders who might have got thus far; and on the inner side of the tower are the stone corbels which formerly supported a timber gallery above the gateway, from which defenders could again assail determined attackers if they gained admission to the court-yard. The upper part of this gate-tower, with its conical-roofed caphouse, is a late 16th-century embellishment. This caphouse gives access to a flat parapet and platform at the top. There is a walk along the crest of the curtain-wall, reached from the upper storey of the tower.

Despite all this defensive strength, however many previous sieges the castle may have withstood, that which made it so famous, as enshrined in the poem about the Bonnie Hoose, seems to have been an exceedingly feeble affair, from the defenders' point of view. In 1640 the Earl of Argyll with 4,000 Covenanting troops and a ruthless Commission of Fire and Sword from the Committee of Estates, came sweeping across Scotland from the west and descended in fury upon the Braes of Angus. Presumably he had some special bone to pick with the Ogilvys. It so happened that the Earl of Airlie was away in England, and his son, the Lord Ogilvy, is reported to have fled at the Campbells' approach. At anyrate Argyll won the day, plundered, burned and attempted to

demolish Airlie Castle, it is said himself 'taking hammer in hand and knocking down the hewed work of doors and windows till he did sweat for heat at his work'—a nice picture of malice. Apparently the 10-feet-thick curtain-walling however was too much even for his Covenanting zeal, and there it stands today.

The castle has recently been fully restored and is once again the seat of the Earl of Airlie, after having stood empty for some time.

ALDBAR CASTLE

Aldbar is an interesting and unusual house of imposing dimensions dating from the late 16th century, unfortunately with large Victorian Gothic additions. It stands in a romantic site of the steep bank of a stream above the Den of Aldbar, two miles west of Brechin, in a finely wooded estate.

On my first glimpse of this fortalice I was struck by certain similarities to Glamis Castle. Glamis, of course, is infinitely larger and more ambitious in every way, but there are certain very significant and unusual details—such as the long, slender angle-turrets with the three windows apiece, the high parapeted stair-tower, and the handsome heraldic panels—which convey a notable resemblance. It therefore came as no surprise to learn that while Glamis itself was given its present aspect mainly by John,

[96]

8th Lord Glamis, Aldbar was built by his brother, Sir Thomas Lyon, Master of Glamis.

It is a tall red sandstone house of four storeys and a garret, with a still taller stair-tower in the re-entrant angle, and corner-turrets crowning certain of the walls. An unusual semi-circular excrescence, which I can only describe as a bulge, rises on the east front over two or three storeys, this being provided with a large gun-loop at the foot, indicating that it is no modern feature. Obviously the ground level has been altered here; in fact the entire site is a difficult one, sloping steeply in more than one direction—although this enhances the defensive possibilities. The windows on this east side are still provided with their iron yetts. The entrance would lie in the foot of the stair-tower, to the west, but this has been engulfed by the modern Gothic front. The main entrance is now to the east. The huge chimney-stack to the left of the sketch is modern, but the other chimneys seen are original. Internally there has inevitably been much alteration.

The aforementioned 8th Lord Glamis purchased Aldbar from the Cramond family in 1577, and gave it to his brother Thomas. Sir Thomas Lyon, Master of Glamis as he is known to history—for he was long heir to his brother—was a harsh and vigorous man who took a prominent part in the murky politics of his day, the youthful years of James the Sixth. His brother Glamis was Chancel-

lor of Scotland and he himself became Lord Treasurer, being one of the fiery Regent Morton's supporters. He was one of the leaders of the Raid of Ruthven when the boy King was kidnapped and immured in Ruthven Castle and forced to sign orders for the dismissal and banishment of his dear friend and cousin Esme, Duke of Lennox, then ruling Scotland, and also of his later favourite the Earl of Arran. On that tearful occasion the Master of Glamis is reported as grimly telling his monarch 'Better bairns weep than grown men!' After James's escape, he fell into disfavour not unnaturally, but later came back into prominence—and the Treasurer-ship once more. He left no son, despite successive marriages, and his nephew the 9th Lord Glamis and first Earl of Kinghorne sold Aldbar to a cadet of the noble house of Sinclair.

The Sinclair lairdship did not last long, and Aldbar passed first to the Young family of Dundee and than to the Chalmers of Balnacraig in Aberdeenshire, a line said to derive from the Clan Cameron, who have remained in possession down to modern times.

NOTE: The author regrets to hear that this castle has been demolished since the above was written.

BALFOUR CASTLE

The single, substantial round tower attached to the more modern farmhouse is all that remains of the large castle of Balfour, said to have been built by the celebrated Cardinal Beaton for one of his mistresses. It stands on rising ground four miles west of Kirriemuir. The tower has a peculiar lean-to roof, presumably an ancient alteration, and appears to have constituted the south-west angle of a courtyard-type castle, traces of which extend to north and east. Six storeys high, it is massively built, its walling being divided by three stringcourses, showing some architectural pretensions, the tower having a distinct taper. Wide gunloops defend its outer aspect. The basement is vaulted, and originally was reached from the courtyard; the present doorway thereto, slapped through from the south, is modern.

The story is that Beaton built this castle for Marion, daughter of the first Lord Ogilvy, his most favoured mistress, and her numerous offspring. Certainly Marion was known as his 'chief lewd' and it has been said that he was actually married to her before he became priest, thereafter reducing her status on his taking holy orders. Certainly she remained a charge on the Abbey's revenues for life. But the Ogilvys possessed Balfour long before Beaton's time. The probability is that the castle was built by the lady's brother Walter, and was extended and enhanced by the Cardinal for Marion and her brood. At anyrate, the Ogilvys retained Balfour for a long period. It passed later to the Fotheringhams.

BRAIKIE CASTLE

This moşt typical late 16th-century laird's house stands beside a modern farmhouse three miles east of Friockheim, and unfortunately has fallen on evil days. It is tall and L-shaped, of four storeys and a garret, with a stair-turret rising above first-floor level in the re-entrant and an angle-turret, now roofless, crowning the south-west gable. Features are the tall chimney-stack which rises beside the stair-turret, and the large number of shot-holes—one in the sill of practically every window. The door is in the re-entrant, protected by an iron yett and wide splayed gunloops. Above is a panel with the arms of Fraser impaling Kinnaird, the initials T.F. and C.K., dated 1581.

The main wide stair rises in the wing of the L to first floor only, the turret stair continuing. The ground floor contains two vaulted cellars, and a small guardroom contrived below the stair. The Hall, on the first floor, is a good-sized chamber, with a private

[99]

stair in the thickness of the wall up to the wing above the stairhead, where was the laird's private room.

The Thomas Fraser who almost certainly built the tower in
1581 was a son of the 5th Lord Lovat, the Lovat Frasers having
been in possession of these lands as early as 1407. In the mid-17th
century they passed to the great Angus family of Gray and at a
still later date to the even greater Ogilvys.

It is unfortunate that this excellent example of its kind should
be in so neglected a condition.

BROUGHTY CASTLE

Rising proudly from its rocky peninsula of Broughty Craig,
thrusting out into the Tay estuary three miles east of Dundee,
Broughty Castle is a well-known landmark. Both architecturally
and historically the castle has had a very chequered career. Today
it has the aspect of a fortress, a military strength, rather than a
fortalice or private semi-fortified house—and indeed it is occupied
by the Army, with much War Office building and excrescence to
mar its lines, in consequence. Nevertheless, the tall, dominant
centre of it all is the old keep built by the Lords Gray in the late
15th and early 16th centuries.

This original work consists of a massive square free-standing
tower, rising five storeys out of a clutter of later building, to a
parapet, with a much-altered garret storey above. The walls, now
harled over, are thick and the windows small. The stairway rises

in the thickness of the south-west angle, and ends in a little gabled caphouse which gives access to the parapet-walk—as seen in sketch. The parapet itself is crenellated and provided with a number of machicolations, or corbelled-out projections, from which pitch, boiling water, and so on, could be dropped in the usual fashion upon unapproved visitors.

Inevitably, internally there has been a great deal of alteration over the centuries, in view of the castle's many vicissitudes. It was in a ruinous state and near collapse in 1842, but in 1855 the Government bought it and restored it as a fortress for coastal defence. Whom the statesmen of the day were intending to defend the Tay estuary against is not clear.

Andrew, 3rd Lord Gray, of Fowlis and Castle Huntly, acquired the lands of Broughty in 1490 and commenced the erection of the fortalice. The date 1496 is said to have appeared formerly on an angle of the tower. The Earl of Crawford refers to it, in 1514, as 'the new fortalice of Broughty'. New or not, it had not long to await excitements. During the Regency of Mary of Guise, the English under Somerset invaded Scotland, and Patrick 4th Lord Gray, commencing the career of treachery for which this family became notorious, met the invaders at St. Andrews and agreed to deliver up his castle of Broughty. For this, eventually, he was arrested, imprisoned in Edinburgh, but at length released. A Minute of the Scots Privy Council of 1547 says 'our auld ynemies of England hes, by way of deid, takin the craig and place of

Broughty and ramforcat them'. Also, 'Our auld ynemies being in the hous of Broughty are apperandly to invaid the burc of Dundie and haill cuntrie, and to burn, herey, sla and destroy . . . etc.' To remedy this state of affairs, the Council ordered 300 men to be raised, 100 of them to be hagbutters, another 100 spearmen, one half to be equipped by the superior clergy at a levy of £600 and the other half by the inhabitants of Dundee, besides 100 horsemen at the joint expense of the counties of Perth, Angus and the Mearns. However, the English garrison numbered 2,000 men—Broughty Craig, which is not very large, must have been crowded in those days—and they were not dislodged for over two years. The castle was then partly demolished. Nine years later, however, the Duke of Chatelherault, chief of the Hamiltons, took possession in the name of the Lords of the Congregation and held Broughty until 1571, when it was captured by Seton of Parbroath in the Popish interests. Thereafter the castle seems to have entered into a period of peace and decline, until the mid-19th century.

CARESTON CASTLE

Standing well back in a large estate, but visible from the main A.94 highway, about five miles west of Brechin, Careston is one of those two-faced houses which tell a different story depending upon from which side it is viewed. From the front it appears to be an imposing example of the tall, symmetrical laird's house of the early 18th century, outwith the fortified period. But from the back and sides the earlier fortalice appears, revealing a lofty tower-house of probably the late 16th century, rising out of a clutter of later building. The best view is from the west, as in sketch. Unfortunately there has been some alteration of this superstructure also, with the stair-turret and angle-turrets losing their conical roofs and being finished with sham crenellations; but the aspect of the original Z-planned house may be discerned fairly clearly, four storeys and a garret in height. The masonry is the local warm red rubble, and there has been considerable elaboration in decorative stonework and corbelling, stringcourses and window-surrounds.

The building is said to contain as nucleus the remains of the 15th-century castle of Caraldston. The early 18th-century front is very impressive, with its tall gabled corner-towers, steep roofs, arcaded basement storey, ornamental stonework and heraldry.

The office of heritable Dempster or Adjudicator to the Scots Parliament was confirmed to Andrew Dempster of Careston by

Robert the Second in 1379. The fifth of this line was of a lawless
character, despite his office, and continually in trouble, especially
with the Bishop of Brechin over disputed lands and grazings,
lifting cattle and horses and once even assisting at the kidnapping
of 'twa monkis'. His son was the last Dempster of Careston,
whereafter the property fell to various families beginning with
the Lindsays at the very end of the 16th century. It would appear
therefore that the earlier portions of the castle are of Dempster
construction. From the Lindsays, Careston passed to Sir Alexander Carnegie, brother of the first Earl of Southesk, and in 1707
Sir John Stewart of Grandtully purchased the estate. He it was
who rebuilt the great south front, and his arms, with the date 1714
still decorate that facade.

CARSE GRAY

Delightfully situated on a terrace site above the wide carseland
two miles north of Forfar, Carse Gray at first sight seems to be a
pleasant homogeneous house of the 18th century, whitewashed,
rambling, E-shaped as to plan, consisting of a long main block
lying east and west, with wings projecting southwards at either
end. Closer inspection, however, reveals that part of the east wing
represents a small and simple but attractive laird's house of probably the early 17th century, T-planned, to which the later house
has been attached. With roughcast walls rising to two storeys and
a garret, the only outer features of this otherwise plain structure

[103]

are in the wing, the roof of which is slightly lower than that of the main block—all of the roof levels here having been almost certainly altered. The upper storey of this wing projects slightly on simple continuous corbelling on the north and south sides, and has done formerly on the west also. The doorway, with moulded surround, is in the north re-entrant, and above is an empty panel-space, also moulded. The two windows of this wing, which was the stair-tower of the original house, are notably smaller than elsewhere.

Internally there has been great alteration to make the main block an integral part of the later house. The turnpike stair still rises to the first floor however, and at this level a curious slantwise recess is contrived in the walling at the south re-entrant, probably to give access to a former shot-hole to defend the approach. The roof lowering has altered the floor levels here, but two moulded stone fireplaces of early construction are still in the walling at former second-floor level. The present laird, in recent restorations, has uncovered these hitherto hidden evidences of the ancient house.

The barony of Carse early belonged to a family named Rynd. In 1621, John Rynd was served heir to his grandfather, William Rynd of Carse, but in 1648 the estate was sold to Colonel Francis Ruthven. In 1741 Charles Gray, son of Gray of Balbunno in Perthshire, a cadet branch of the Lords Gray, acquired the property and changed the name to Carse Gray. His descendants are still in possession.

CLAYPOTTS CASTLE

The unusual appearance of Claypotts Castle attracts a good deal of attention and comment, especially the effect of the vigorous corbelling-out of the tops of its two rounded towers to square watch-chambers with gabled roofs. This, of course, is a quite common feature in fortalices of the period, on one tower; but it is less usual to see it on two; also the dimensions of these cap-like watch-chambers are unusual.

Claypotts stands about one mile to the north-west of Broughty Ferry, now amongst the outskirts of Dundee. Despite its elaborate aspect, the planning is fairly simple, consisting of an oblong main block lying north and south, with large circular towers at the north-east and south-west angles. These towers do not contain stairways; the stairs, of the usual turnpike variety, rise in smaller semi-circular stair-towers contrived in the angles between the large towers and the main block, one at either side. One of them can be seen to the right of the sketch. The main building rises to three storeys and a garret, with the towers a storey higher, the walls being liberally sprinkled with gunloops and shot-holes. An interesting point, not at first obvious, is that the two squared-off watch-chambers are differently sized, though seemingly identical. Indeed, they were built probably at twenty-year intervals by a father and son.

There is a great deal of accommodation in a plan of this type, with smaller rooms housed in each of the round towers to supplement the main block apartments. Altogether there is a basement kitchen and three cellars on the ground floor, a large public room on each upper floor, with the Hall on the first, and eight smaller chambers in the towers. There are tiny battlements at garret level at each gable of the main block, though these have lost their parapets—an unusual feature.

Claypotts is a house of the late 16th century, one of the enormous number which sprang up all over Scotland on the sharing out of the vast church lands at the Reformation. Two dates are carved on gables of the two watch-chambers, that to the south 1569; the other 1588—the 5, curiously enough, being shown upside-down. Also on the north gable is a shield with the arms of Strachan and the initials I.S.

The lands were granted by Alexander Third to the Abbey of Lindores, and remained church property until the Reformation when they were acquired by Gilbert Strathauchtyne, or Strachan, in 1560. Presumably Gilbert began the building of the castle, and

it was finished by his son John. From the Strachans Claypotts passed to the Grahams of Claverhouse in 1625, but at the forfeiture of 'Bloody Clavers', Viscount Dundee, it passed to the Earls of Angus and the Douglases. The story that this was one of the many castles built by Cardinal Beaton for one of his mistresses is obviously false, since Beaton died many years before Claypotts was built. A legend of a drudging brownie clings to this house— one of those useful supernatural domestics said to have haunted certain fortunate Scots establishments. This one is supposed to have been driven away by the dogged hostility of a female servant who apparently did not know when she was lucky.

COLLISTON CASTLE

This most interesting house, standing on the Brothock Water four miles north-west of Arbroath, is a 16th-century fortalice on the Z-plan, consisting of a main block with round towers projecting at diagonally opposite corners, and with a massive stair-turret rising in one of the re-entrant angles so formed. One of the round towers is corbelled-out to the square at the top, so that the entire plan is very similar to that of Claypotts Castle in the same county —although the houses at first glance do not show much resemblance. The structure, however, has been much altered in the 17th century and in modern times. McGibbon and Ross's illustration, in their excellent *Castellated and Domestic Architecture of Scotland* shows a much plainer house than we see today.

The walls, which are harled and pink-washed, rise to three storeys and an attic. The present parapet and open rounds, however, are modern, and the entire upper storey has been altered— most notably in the smaller round tower, which was originally corbelled-out to the square like its neighbour but is now finished off in unconvincing fashion with flat roof and parapet. This modern tower-head should in fact be slightly higher than seen in the sketch, which was made under difficult conditions. Interesting external features of the main building are the peculiar stringcourse part-framing the second-floor windows, and the ample provision of wide splayed gunloops and circular shot-holes. Also the amusing little lambs' heads which support the sill of the main tower first-floor window.

The entrance is in the foot of this main tower, flanked by gun-loops. This almost certainly would be the original entrance, but McGibbon and Ross's sketch shows the door sited in the centre of the main block. This door is again now built up to a window. Over it is a panel bearing the royal arms of Scotland with the initials I.R. for James Sixth, dated 1621. Also the initials H.G. and I.L., plus the motto LAVS DEO. This motto appears again on the stair-turret, above the original doorway, with the Guthrie and Falconer arms and initials I.G. and M.F., dated 1553—almost certainly referring to the original builder John Guthrie, and his wife. The other panel, with the initials H.G. no doubt refer to Henry Guthrie who would be responsible for the 17th-century alterations. This Sir Henry was Crouner or Coroner of Arbroath, which office, it is suggested would account for the royal arms being used here. The present dormer pediments are modern. Certain carved stones built into the front walling are interesting, and are thought possibly to represent relics of a former Culdee temple nearby.

Internally, the ground floor is vaulted, the kitchen as usual being the basement chamber furthest from the main doorway. The principal turnpike stair almost certainly rose in the foot of the main tower, to first floor, the ascent thereafter being continued by the turret stair; but this has been replaced by a squared scale-and-platt stair in a central projection to the rear. The Hall, on the first floor, is a fine room, with a private stair in the thickness of the wall leading down to the laird's wine-cellar below, now built up. The first-floor windows were enlarged in the 17th century.

Colliston is one of the many castles associated with the potent Cardinal Beaton. As Abbot of Arbroath he gave a charter of the lands to John Guthrie and Isabella Ogilvy his wife in 1542. His

own most favoured mistress and 'chief lewd' was Marion Ogilvy, and quite likely Isabella was their daughter. A room in the house is still known as Beaton's Room. Sir Henry Guthrie sold Colliston in the late 17th century to a Dr Gordon, and in 1721 it was acquired by George Chaplin, with whose descendants it remained until comparatively modern times.

CORTACHY CASTLE

This famous house occupies a delightful setting within a bend of the rushing River South Esk just where it issues from the Grampian foothills into the great plain of Strathmore, some four miles north of Kirriemuir. Although it has been greatly altered and extended down the centuries, it stems from a courtyard-type castle of probably the 15th century, of which three of the circular flanking towers still remain, with portions of the curtain-walling between which has been raised and incorporated in to the later building. The fourth and main tower, or keep, has presumably been overwhelmed in all the extensions to the north and east. The view as sketched shows the only more or less unaltered portion, in the tower to the left, corbelled out to the square at its top storey to house a typical gabled watch-chamber—unfortunately with unsuitable 'Tudor-type' tall chimneys superimposed. The upper works of the tower to the right are modern, as is the entire roofline of the range between. The remaining circular tower is out of view to the west. The manner in which the watch-chamber is corbelled-

[108]

out is unusual; this is probably a late 16th or early 17th-century addition to the tower.

There being at least six periods of building represented in Cortachy, it is impossible to give any coherent description of the internal arrangements. There was a castle here in the 14th century, but of this no trace remains. It then belonged to the Earls of Strathearn, of the Stewart line. In 1473 King James the Third granted Cortachy to Sir Walter Ogilvy of Oures, and it seems likely that he it was who built the nucleus of the existing castle. He lost Cortachy, however, to a kinsman, Thomas Ogilvy of Clova, whose descendants held it until 1625 when it was bought by still another branch of the great Ogilvy family, in the person of the first Earl of Airlie. He was a famous Royalist and supporter of King Charles the First, and in consequence his Castle of Airlie was ravaged and part destroyed by the Covenanting party under the Earl of Argyll—whereupon the family moved to Cortachy. Additions and alterations were made at this time. King Charles Second spent a night here in 1650, in what is still known as the King's Room, now the panelled dining-room. The following year Cortachy was sacked by Cromwell's troops in consequence. The son and heir of the family, who became second Earl, had also fought and suffered much for the royal cause, but despite being sentenced to death for his share in the Battle of Philiphaugh, with Montrose, he lived to the age of ninety-three. Three generations later, his great-grandson was forfeited for once more supporting

the House of Stewart in the Rising of 1745, but the lands and title were eventually restored to his nephew as 7th Earl in 1826. He, having married a wealthy heiress, was responsible for the greatest of the enlargements and alterations to the castle, although his successor, the 8th Earl also extended it when he employed the well-known Victorian architect, David Bryce, noted for his 'Scottish-Baronial' profusions then becoming fashionable as a result of Queen Victoria's popularising of Balmoral and the Scottish theme.

Today, the Ogilvy family are still at Cortachy, although the Earl of Airlie lives at Airlie Castle, restored again, not far away, and it is his son and heir, Lord Ogilvy, who occupies this historic house at the mouth of Glen Clova.

CRAIG CASTLE

Craig, occupying a pleasant position on a high ridge of ground overlooking Montrose Basin from the south, is an interesting and most unusual series of buildings of highly individual planning. First of all there is a massive and impressive gatehouse group, leading into a very large rectangular forecourt or outer bailey, situated at right-angles to the castle proper. Although ruinous and ivy-covered this is a most interesting feature, with flanking drum-towers, an arched gateway between them with corbelled machicolations of what has been a watch-chamber above, and it seems, a parapet and walk stretching between the drum-towers, all well protected by gunloops. High walls and the mass of the house itself enclose the remainder of the courtyard.

The house consists of two small square parapeted towers, sturdy and strong, probably of the 15th century, linked by another high wall with parapet and walk. These form the south side of the square, the west and north sides comprising two ranges of building of later date, probably of the 17th century but clearly built on the foundations of earlier work. The east side opens on to the outer forecourt and has been separated from it by another wall.

The two square towers which are very similar in appearance but not identical, are three storeys and a garret in height, the parapet of the eastern one being plain, while that to the west is crenellated. Each has a little garret chamber with crowstepped gables within the parapet-walk. Almost certainly, originally, there would be similar square towers at the other two corners of the inner courtyard, although that to the north-west might well be considerably larger, to form the main keep of the castle. The base-

[110]

ments are vaulted, the windows tiny, and the east tower has vestiges of an arched inner gateway to the courtyard, with crooks for the iron yett and socket-holes for timber bars.

The inhabited part of the house is fairly plain, three storeys high with semi-dormer windows. Modern additions have been made to the north wing, which do not improve it, and many windows have been enlarged. The door is in the main west wing and appears to have been moved a yard or two north of its previous position. Inset in the walling of this front are four panels. One has been over the earlier door and bears the date 1637. The others, much worn, are heraldic and bear the initials D.S.C. The north wing is vaulted, containing four chambers, that to the east being the kitchen. The next cellar to it has a tiny staircase rising in the thickness of the wall to the first floor room which would be the Hall, the access being to the laird's wine-cellar. The vaulting of the west wing has been removed.

Craig Castle, which is still occupied, was a possession of the Carnegie family, cadets of the Earls of Southesk. Craig was renowned as a strong castle and was frequently mentioned by Scottish chroniclers.

Early proprietors of Craig were the Woods—or as they were previously known, the De Bosco family—of Norman origin. Sir David Wood of Craig was Comptroller of Scotland under James Fifth. Since they were still in possession in 1617, it was the Woods who built the original castle. Soon after, however, Craig was acquired by David Carnegie, 1st Earl of Southesk who settled it on his second son Sir James around 1626. He eventually succeeded to the earldom and Craig went to his younger brother, married to Jane, daughter of Sir John Scrymgeour of Dudhope, Constable of Dundee—who, for some unstated reason, obtained special permission from the Lords of the Privy Council to eat flesh in Lent. It is worth noting that the sister of these two lairds of Craig, the Lady Magdalene Carnegie, married in 1629 James, the great Earl and later Marquis of Montrose.

DUDHOPE CASTLE

This large castle, ancient seat of the Scrymgeours, Constables of Dundee, now grievously altered, debased and fallen on evil days, still retains some vestiges of its proud past as it stands on high ground looking out over the roof-tops of the city. It has suffered much at the hands of time, neglect, vandals and improvers, but still survives threats to demolishment. Surely the city of Dundee will find some worthy use for this once-handsome monument to her stirring past?

The building has inevitably undergone great changes in appearance, for it has been used as a barracks and a woollen factory. The original fortalice was probably an oblong tower, to which wings were added to form an L-plan, this now being represented by that portion of the structure in the sketch, nearest to the viewer—that is, the south-east corner. But at a fairly early date Dudhope was converted to the more ambitious courtyard or palace plan, with the rise in importance of the Scrymgeour family. Two sides of the courtyard still remain, to south and east. Whether the north and west sides were ever completed, or were merely enclosed by curtain-walling, is not clear. Round towers with conical roofs command the angles, with splayed gunloops in their bases. A little stair-turret connects third and fourth floors in the angle of the south-west tower. The north-east tower has a tall chimney-stack rising from it, which is unusual—but can be seen also at Earlshall in Fife.

The entrance lies between two drum-towers which have been foreshortened, in the centre of the east front. The gablet and belfry surmounting these are modern. The roof-level of both wings has been raised, which has not improved the looks of the building. The upper windows were formerly dormers, and would appear much more attractive.

The arched entrance pend leads into what was formerly an enclosed court. Here, the corbelling of what has been another stair-turret alone remains projecting from the face of the south wing.

Over one of the courtyard windows is the date 1660. The building as a whole, of course, is older than this.

Within the entrance passage is a recessed space for the guard. The old stairway, wide and square, is reached from a moulded stone doorway just to the left, inside the courtyard, and gives access to all floors. A vaulted passage runs along the inner side of the main south wing, from which opens a range of vaulted cellars, which, owing to the fall of the ground level to the south are almost semi-subterranean. At the west end this passage leads into a large kitchen with a great arched fireplace provided with its own window. The south-west tower has its own outer door and contains a wide circular stair rising to the upper floors. There has been an enormous amount of internal alteration, window enlargement, and so on. The building is at present not in very good condition.

William Wallace, as Governor of the Realm of Scotland, conferred the lands, with the title of hereditary Constable of Dundee, on his lieutenant Alexander Scrymgeour in 1298. Dudhope remained with his descendants until 1668. Over two windows of the east front are panels depicting the arms and monograms of Dame Magdalen Livingstone, of the family of Linlithgow and Callander, but no date. She was wife to Sir James Scrymgeour. James the Sixth visited Dudhope in 1617. Sir John Scrymgeour, the 11th Constable, was created Viscount Dudhope in 1641. James, 2nd Viscount was mortally wounded fighting for King Charles First at Marston Moor. John, 3rd Viscount and 13th Constable was created Earl of Dundee, and though the earldom went into abeyance for a long period, it has of recent years been restored to Henry J. Scrym-geour-Wedderburn, former Under-Secretary of State for Scotland.

It would be pleasing and apt if this ancient home of the family could likewise see a modern restoration.

EDZELL CASTLE

Situated amongst Grampian foothills seven miles north of Brechin, Edzell is a notable former stronghold of the famous family of Lindsay, Earls of Crawford, so long powerful in Scottish history. A quite complex series of buildings, it occupies a strategic position at the junction of two ancient crossing routes of the Mounth.

The structure includes an extensive range of buildings linked by two great enclosures—the actual courtyard and a still larger pleasaunce, something more than a walled garden, with its own subsidiary buildings. This latter is the major glory of Edzell. Its Lodge, or Summer-house, which acts as a corner-tower to this enclosure, is still entire, although the main castle buildings are ruinous. The sketch shows this Lodge, with keep in the background.

This keep, the oldest portion of the castle, dates from the early 16th century, replacing an earlier castle. It is oblong on plan, with a slightly projecting stair-tower, rising four storeys to a parapet, which has now gone, as has the garret storey above. The walls are of red freestone coursed rubble, and the parapet, which was supported on a double table of individual and continuous corbelling, has been provided with open rounds at all angles, with a projecting half-round, for added defence, in the centre of each front. A caphouse surmounted the stairhead at the northern angle. Wide splayed gunloops open at basement level on all fronts.

An arched doorway from the courtyard, in the re-entrant, gives access to the two vaulted cellars of the basement, that to the east having a private stair in the thickness of the wall to the Hall above and no doubt being the wine-cellar. The Hall is a handsome apartment measuring 33 by 23 feet, lit by two windows, one with stone seats. There is a fine fireplace, seven feet wide, and a smaller one at the east end, indicating that this area has been screened off. There are mural chambers, one eleven feet in length. The upper floors have been subdivided by timber partitions to provide ample sleeping accommodation. The stair is roomy, with five-feet-wide steps.

To east and north of the keep has been added, in the late 16th century, a large L-shaped range, now very ruinous, three storeys high, with gabled roof but no parapet. A large circular tower projects at the west angle, for flank defence of the walling, and a semi-circular stair-tower has risen in the main re-entrant. The remainder of the courtyard has been enclosed by curtain-walling, the entrance being by an arched gateway and pend slapped through the south-west front.

The pleasaunce, to the south-east, was added in the early 17th century by Sir David Lindsay, Lord Edzell, of Session, whose arms, with those of his wife, Dame Isabel Forbes, and their initials, surmount a gateway, dated 1604. He was a son of the 9th Earl, a much travelled and cultured man. The pleasaunce measures 172 by 143 feet, the twelve-foot-high walls being highly decorative and ornamented by a wonderful series of sculptured stone panels representing the Planetary Deities, the Liberal Arts and the Cardinal Virtues, based on designs from Nuremburg where Lord Edzell had visited.

The Lodge at the eastern corner is a delightful self-contained, two-storeyed house, oblong, with its own stair-tower, angle-turret, and gunloops for defence. Upper windows have handsome tympana and triple shot-holes of varied design in their breasts. The moulded doorway is in the foot of the stair-tower, but a modern door has been opened nearby. The basement contains two vaulted chambers, one groined. The upper apartment, reached by a wide turnpike, has been subdivided in modern times, and has a decorative fireplace and aumbry. At the south angle of the pleasaunce, has been another corner tower in the form of a bath-house.

The Lindsays gained Edzell in 1357 by marriage with the heiress of Glenesk, Catherine Stirling. Here Mary Queen of Scots stayed and held a Privy Council in 1562, on her one expedition into the Highlands. Cromwell garrisoned the castle in 1651. The Lindsay ownership ended in 1715, with debts of £192,502 Scots, when the Earl of Panmure bought the property. This family was forfeited after the Jacobite Rising, but managed to re-purchase the estate in 1764. It is now in the care of the Ministry of Works.

ETHIE CASTLE

The extensive and handsome mansion of Ethie, for centuries the seat of the Carnegie Earls of Northesk, is difficult adequately to describe owing to its great size and many ramifications and extensions, most of them of an early date. The nucleus, however, appears to have been a large square keep, substantially of the 15th century, though probably incorporating still older work, which now forms the south-western corner of a great and roughly rectangular mass of building. A modern balustraded tower has been raised above this, unfortunately, hiding the original line, and the entire roof-level has been altered and modernised. The earliest extension of the old fortalice, however, dating probably from the mid-16th century, is more or less unaltered externally, as illustrated. It is plainly discernible, a four-storeyed L-shaped block rising to the east, its wing a stair-tower off-set on continuous corbelling at two levels, with a doorway opening at its base. To the left of the sketch are the lower storeys of the original castle.

Other extensions of the late 16th and 17th centuries reach out to north and west, to form a large and complicated rectangle, with inner and outer courtyards, too intricate for description here. The original keep was surrounded by a barmekin or curtain-wall with flanking towers, and some of this has been incorporated in the later extensions, notably the round tower at the north-west angle, to the left of the main entrance. In this three filled-in gunloops and a shot-hole may still be traced.

The present main entrance, which was formerly a gateway through the curtain-wall, is surmounted by a worn heraldic panel. The door now leads directly into the house. The ground floor of the keep contains three vaulted cellars, the westernmost of which has a private stair in the thickness of the walling giving access to what was the Hall above—a common arrangement for the laird's convenience in the matter of either wine-cellar or prisoners' cell. The massive chimney-stack which rises to the east indicates that

[116]

the vault at that end would be the original kitchen. This has been complemented or superseded by another kitchen in the eastern range, with great arched fireplace and a well, dating probably from the late 16th century.

Near the outer courtyard entrance on the north front is a 'louping-on stane' or mounting-block, into which has been built a heraldic pediment, no doubt from a dormer window, now much defaced. The entire building was formerly surrounded by a moat, traces of which still exist to the north-east. It was obviously a place of strength.

Ethie was inhabited by Cardinal Beaton when he was Abbot of Arbroath, about 1530, and again later when Cardinal and Archbishop, between 1538 and 1546, and so must have witnessed much making of the bloody history of these unhappy days, when the Reformation was being held down with fire and sword. Even at that time it was said to be a fortress of considerable antiquity. It passed to Sir Robert Carnegie in 1549, and his grandson Sir John, High Sheriff of Forfar, was created Lord Lour and Earl of Ethie in 1649, which titles he exchanged after the Restoration for those of Baron Rosehill and Inglismaldie and Earl of Northesk. The 7th Earl was a distinguished admiral and third in command at the Battle of Trafalgar. Other members of the family also made their mark on history.

Ethie, though no longer the home of the Northesk family is still occupied and carefully cherished in excellent order.

Farnell, four miles south of Brechin, is particularly interesting because its eastern portion (to right of sketch) represents the original palace of the Bishops of Brechin—in 1512 Bishop Meldrum refers to it as 'Palatium Nostrum'—and a tiny palace it has been. The remainder of the main block and the stair-tower were added after the Reformation when the building became a secular fortalice for the new owner of the lands, Catherine, Countess of Crawford.

The building, not unnaturally, has certain unusual features; the large gabled crowsteps of the ecclesiastical portion; a projecting garderobe and sanitary flues on the north front; the double row of corbels on the east gable to support a former timber gallery; the tiny carved shields of the northern skewputts, with the monogram I.M. for Jesu Maria and M. surmounted by a heavenly crown. In the later extension the fashion in which the stair-tower is corbelled-out to the square so high up as to seem hardly worth-while is interesting; as is the peculiar buttresslike erection near the west end of the south wall, with crenellations, the purpose of which appears to be merely to thicken the wall here to contain a wall-closet—extraordinary lengths to go to for so humdrum an end. The doorway, in the foot of the stair-tower, is guarded by shot-holes. Internally the house has been much altered. A Ministry of Works grant has recently been made towards restoration. The basement is not vaulted. Farnell came eventually to the family of the Earl of Southesk by purchase.

FINAVON CASTLE

The formerly great and important castle stands in a strong position where the Lemno Burn joins the South Esk five miles north-
north-east of Forfar. A stronghold of the Earls of Crawford, the
original establishment, dating from the 14th century, must have
been extensive, but all that now remains is a single tall and massive
tower, 86 feet high, soaring above various basement foundations.
The upper works of this appear to date from no earlier than the
16th century, although the lower storeys are probably older. This
tower, still complete to the wallhead at the north and east sides,
is only a broken shell elsewhere. It has been L-shaped, five storeys
and a garret high, the wing projecting westwards. A large 16th-
century angle-turret, with double shot-holes, enhances the north-
east angle, beside the massive chimney-stack of the crowstepped
gable, and the wallhead is topped by an ornamental eaves-course.
At this level in the re-entrant angle the corbelling of another turret projects, probably a stair-turret to the caphouse or watch-
chamber. The east front, weakened by the regular succession of
fairly large windows one above another, is badly riven. In con-
trast, the north front has no single aperture of any sort—an unusual feature. The masonry is good coursed red sandstone rubble,
and the lower storeys well provided with 15th-century gunloops.

The basement is vaulted and still provided with its massive
iron-studded oaken door. All the other floors have fallen in and
details are no longer discernible. At the top of the tower, to the
south-east, are said to remain the iron hooks from which Earl
Beardie hanged the minstrel who foretold his defeat at the Battle
of Brechin in 1452.

The history of Finavon would fill volumes. Held by the Lindsays from 1375, here David, 3rd Earl and his foeman brother-in-
law Ogilvy of Inverquharity were both brought, sore wounded,
from the Battle of Arbroath in 1446. The Earl died within a week,
whereupon his Countess hurried to her own brother's sick-room
and smothered him with a pillow. Their son Alexander was that
potent and savage 4th Earl, The Tiger, or Earl Beardie, whose
cruelties were notorious even for that age. In rebellion against
James the Second, he fled to Finavon from the rout of Brechin
declaring that he would gladly pass seven years in hell to gain the
victory over Huntly the victor. James was persuaded to pardon
him, and came here to be sumptuously entertained by the former
rebel. Having previously sworn 'to make the highest stone of
Finavon the lowest', the King had to go through the motions of

casting down a loose stone from the topmost battlements to the ground. This stone was long preserved hanging on a chain. On the Covin Tree, reputed to have sprung from a chestnut dropped by a Roman soldier, the Earl hanged Jock Barefoot, a running gillie, for the offence of cutting a walkingstick therefrom. Legend says that this was not the first occasion he mishandled this poor creature; he is supposed to have cut out his tongue for some minor offence, and the poor ghost is alleged still to run between Finavon and Careston Castles trying to deliver his message.

In 1530 the 8th Earl was imprisoned for thirteen weeks in the dungeon of his own castle by his son, known in history as the Wicked Master. So evil were his ways that he was disinherited and superseded by his cousin, the Laird of Edzell, eventually to be stabbed to death in a drunken brawl by a Dundee cobbler. His son was reinstated as 10th Earl. He married at Finavon an illegitimate daughter of Cardinal Beaton and received one of the most handsome dowries in Scottish history.

Finavon passed from the Lindsays in 1629 and was owned by a succession of noble families, Edzell Castle having become the favoured Lindsay seat.

FLEMINGTON HOUSE

Now partly roofless and in a bad state of repair, this is a fairly typical laird's house of probably the early 17th century, standing beside a modern farmhouse near Aberlemno, six miles north-east of Forfar. Three storeys high, it conforms to a variation of the L-plan, whereby there are two re-entrant angles, in each of which rises a stair-turret, the inner one being typically semi-circular and serving all floors above the first, the other being unusual, flat-faced and only carrying a stair between first and second floors. The red sandstone walls are well supplied with gunloops and shot-holes.

The entrance is in the usual inner re-entrant. The basement contains two vaulted chambers, that to the south being the old kitchen with wide arched fireplace. The main turnpike stair rises in the wing only to the first floor, and has beneath it a guard-room with gunloops. The Hall on the first floor has been subdivided at a later date. There has been ample private accommodation above, served by the two turret stairs.

History here is notably scanty. Robert Third granted Flemington to Sir William Dishington. Thereafter I have uncovered nothing until the time of the Reverend John Ochterlony, former episcopal clergyman of the parish, who was repeatedly ejected from the parish church for insisting on taking over the pulpit at services. He continued to minister to his faithful in Flemington Castle, however, until 1742 when his militancy was rewarded by the grant of the Bishopric of Brechin.

FORTER CASTLE

Forter was an outlying stronghold of the great family of Ogilvy of Airlie, situated remotely high up the narrow valley of Glen Isla about twelve miles north of Alyth, undoubtedly maintained both as a convenient refuge from pressing troubles in the populous territories of Strathmore, and also as a protection for the low lands against raids of Highland caterans. The present building appears to date from fairly late in the fortified period, the walls, of rough grey rubble, being of no great thickness. The castle, now very ruinous, is on a variation of the L-plan, with a square stair-wing projecting southwards at a corner of the main block. It is four storeys and a garret in height, a stair-turret projects above first floor in the main re-entrant, and round turrets crown the south-east and south-west angles of the main block. There are a number of small shot-holes.

The entrance is in the foot of the wing, in the re-entrant, and admits to a wide stair to the first floor only, above which the ascent is continued by the turret stair. The basement contained three vaulted chambers, now fallen in, one being the kitchen, provided with a notably wide fireplace, 19 feet across. Above the main stair-head the ceiling was also vaulted, an unusual feature. The Hall on the first floor was commodious, measuring 32 by 19 feet, with a large fireplace to one side, of which only the relieving arch remains. There was another smaller fireplace to the west, with mural chamber adjoining. All floors have now fallen in.

The lands came to the Ogilvys from the Abbey of Coupar, presumably at the Reformation. The castle was plundered and burned by the Earl (later first Marquis) of Argyll, Montrose's enemy, in 1640. The Restoration Committee of Estates' account of this in 1661 says: '... Argyll most cruelly and unhumanly enters the house of Airly and beats the same to the ground and right sua he does to Furtour; syne spoiled all within both houses and such as could not be carried they masterfully brake down and destroyed.' Presumably Forter was largely rebuilt after this incident.

GAGIE HOUSE

This has been a small fortalice of the early 17th century, much added to and altered. Its plan now approximates to the letter T, of which the original portion forms the leg, a little oblong house of two storeys, harled and whitewashed, with two long angle-turrets at the southern gable. There have been alterations to the pitch of the roof, the gable has been widened, and certain windows blocked up while others have been enlarged.

Internally the house has had to suffer like alterations to link up with major modern additions, but the old-world atmosphere is retained, and panelling and ironwork remain. A heraldic panel on the west front shows the arms of Leslie with the initials I.L. There is no date here, but on another armorial panel in the handsome Renaissance summer-house of the walled garden is the date 1614 and the arms of Guthrie. These arms also appeared over the old entrance to the house, with the initials I.G. and T.H., for John

Guthrie of that Ilk and his wife, the daughter of the Reverend James Hodge, minister of Longforgan.

Anciently Oliver lands, Gagie was bought by William Guthrie, second son of Alexander Guthrie of that Ilk in 1610, who presumably built the house. He married Isabella, daughter of Leslie of Balquhain, which no doubt accounts for the first armorial panel mentioned. His grandson Francis, married his cousin Bathia, daughter of Bishop Guthrie who had acquired the family's principal property of Guthrie Castle. Their son in due course inherited both estates, and so became Guthrie of that Ilk.

GARDYNE CASTLE

Gardyne is one of the most unusual and attractive fortalices in a county rich in this class of building. Situated high above a deep ravine a mile south-east of Friockheim, it is a late 16th-century tower to which an extension was added later. Certain authorities date this addition at 1740, but to my eye it looks considerably earlier. Since the Lyell family acquired Gardyne in 1682, and the crest and motto of Lyell of Dysart appears over the present doorway in this extension, I see no reason why this part of the house should not date from that period. There is also a small modern wing, but so placed as not to detract from the ancient appearance of the house.

The original tower has been oblong on plan, with a circular stair-tower rising at the north-east angle; this is corbelled-out to form a square watch-chamber at its top, reached by a tiny turret stair projecting in the re-entrant angle. The two southern angles of the main block are crowned by very elaborate and unusual corner-turrets, such as I have never come across elsewhere. These are most interesting in a number of ways; their conical roofs are of stone, not slate; they terminate in little coronets of masonry; each is provided with a purely decorative parapet, drained by cannon-like spouts, and also a dummy dormer window; and let into the supporting corbelling of each is a form of machicolation for the pouring of boiling water, pitch, or other unpleasantness upon unwelcome visitors—a feature which I have not seen in this form elsewhere in so late a fortalice.

The walls are of the local dark red sandstone, rising to three storeys and a garret, and are well provided with gunloops with squared apertures. The corbelling is very fine throughout, and there is an ornate little window facing north in the watch-cham-

ber. On the west wall of the original portion is a weather-worn
shield, said to depict the arms of Gardyne of Leys, with the date
1568—which aptly seems to represent the period of building.

The later addition is suitably in style, a continuation of the main
block and of similar proportions, more than doubling the accommodation.

Internally the old part of the house has been very little altered.
The basement is vaulted. The Hall on the first floor has a peculiar
square window moulded internally at its jambs, and the interior
of the little watch-chamber is enhanced by rope-moulding and a
tiny fireplace. In the 17th-century wing is much excellent Memel
pine panelling.

Gardyne belonged anciently to the family of the same name
who seem to have been almost permanently at feud with the
neighbouring Guthries of that Ilk, after a daughter of the house
married Guthrie in 1558 and their son, quarrelling with his rela-
tives, was stabbed to death by his Gardyne cousin. Guthrie Castle
is barely two miles away, and the inconvenience of such close-
range hostilities needs no stressing. Eventually the Gardynes seem
to have come off second-best, and of the family there is now no
trace. We read that Patrick Gardyne of that Ilk was slain in 1578
by William Guthrie of that Ilk. Ten years later the Gardynes
achieved success by the slaughter of the Guthrie chief, suffering
prosecution for the deed. In two more years however the Guthries
fell upon the Gardynes and killed the laird and others. This sort
of thing continued over several generations—although presum-

ably the generations were brief ones! In the end, King James Sixth had to intervene—and when that happened, the Crown was apt to be the ultimate beneficiary.

In 1682, at anyrate, Gardyne was acquired by James Lyell, and this family remained in possession until a recent date.

GLAMIS CASTLE

This, of course, is one of the most famous castles, not only in Scotland but in the world. And worthily so, both in its architecture and its history, neither of which can be done justice to in the space at my disposal. Yet however overpowering the impression of grandeur, if we can overlook for a moment all the embellishments and details, the basic plan of Glamis is no more complicated than is the general run of 16th and 17th century Scottish fortalices. It is just the old favourite L-plan, with a circular stair-tower rising in the re-entrant—the most normal and useful design for any fortified house built in stone. A glance at the tall portion of the castle, ignoring all the 'top-hamper' and the lower wings and extensions, and the L-plan becomes quite plain.

The original castle was a 15th century tower, heightened in the 16th century, and added to and extended to east and west a century later still. Undoubtedly there was a famous castle here before the 15th century—the Thane of Glamis in *Macbeth* had his fortalice—but its remains are incorporated in the lower portions of the 15th-century tower. This would rise to the usual parapet, at fourth-floor level, and probably the corbelling of the main angle-turrets would once support open parapet rounds. There are glimpses of the ordinary individual corbels of the parapet still to be seen in the gables. All above that level will date from the two following centuries.

The two massive round towers at the extreme east and west of the lower extensions are all that remain of the flanking towers of a great courtyard for the central keep, the curtain-walling and the other towers of which have been swept away and the flat-roofed wings added.

It is impossible here to attempt any real description of the interior, or of the plentitude of heraldic decoration. Three of the storeys of the original tower were vaulted, with walls ten feet thick. The old kitchen was in the vaulted basement, with a huge fireplace and a well. The first floor, also vaulted, contained the lower or common Hall, 51 by 21 feet, with five windows but,

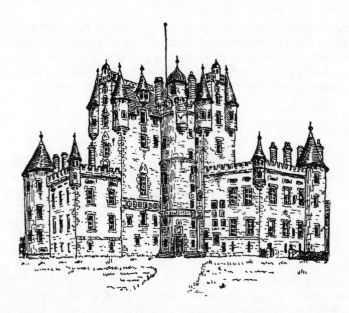

curiously, no fireplace. The Great Hall is on the floor above, a magnificent apartment measuring 54 by 21 feet, with a large fireplace, deep windows, and a mural chamber which communicates with the well two storeys below. There is a wealth of bedrooms above, nine or ten on each floor. The great stairway rises to third-floor level. The lofty roof-promenade is 93 feet above the ground.

The Castle of Glamis, whatever its misty antiquity, was given by King Robert Second, the first of the Stewarts, to Sir John Lyon, Chancellor of Scotland, who married his daughter. Their grandson was created 1st Lord Glamis in 1445. It is still owned by his lineal descendant, some 25 generations later, now Earl of Strathmore and Kinghorne. Patrick, 9th Lord and 1st Earl of Kinghorne, laird from 1578 until 1615 gave the castle its existing main characteristics. His was the impressive 16th-century heightening and also much of the lavish heraldic decoration. His son completed much of the building work and added some excellent plaster ceilings.

The Lyons, one of the most important families in Scotland, frequently provided occupants of the Chancellorship. Their castle inevitably saw many stirring events and had many vicissitudes. The wife of the 6th Lord was burned to death on a trumped-up witchcraft charge of conspiring to poison James Fifth. The 8th Lord, Chancellor, though a most sober individual, was killed in a brawl with Lindsays in a Stirling street in 1578; and his brother, the less admirable Master of Glamis, Lord Treasurer, was one of the main conspirators in kidnapping young James Sixth at the Raid of Ruthven. And so on. Here of course was brought up our gracious Queen-Mother, as Lady Elizabeth Bowes-Lyon.

GUTHRIE CASTLE

A handsome, ancient square tower of the 15th century, round which a modern mansion has grown, set in a fine estate two miles west of Friockheim. The oblong plan has a small stair-wing projecting. Three storeys and an attic high, the tower has a crenellated parapet and open rounds, but this is a modern restoration, as are the pyramidical-roofed caphouse and the attic dormers.

The original entrance, in the centre of the south front, opened into a lobby within the 8-feet thick walling, from which the two basement chambers were reached. To the right rose a straight stair, also in the walling, to the first floor, on which would be the Hall. Above, the turnpike projecting in the wing served the other floors and ended in the caphouse leading to the parapet-walk. In the base of this wing is a tiny chamber, either guardroom or prison.

The building is excellently preserved, and happily still occupied by Guthrie of Guthrie. Its history is lively, feuding with the neighbouring house of Gardyne and others being almost chronic. The keep is said to have been built by Sir David Guthrie, Lord Treasurer and Lord Justice General in 1468, though the Guthries had long been prominent in Scottish affairs. His son fell at Flodden with *his* son and three brothers-in-law. A grandson married a daughter of Gardyne of the Ilk, out of which started the famous feud. Eventually both families lost their lands, but while the Guthries recovered theirs, the Gardynes did not.

HATTON CASTLE

The ruins of this fine late 16th-century mansion lie at the western base of Hatton Hill, commanding the Sidlaw pass of Glack, just above Newtyle. A Z-planned fortalice, it was built by Laurence, 4th Lord Oliphant in 1575. The main block, of three storeys, an attic and a garret, lies east and west, with square towers projecting to north-east and south-west, and circular stair-towers rising in the outer re-entrants thus formed. The walls are liberally provided with shot-holes and gunloops, and the massive chimney-stack of the Hall fireplace is a feature of the inner south front.

The moulded doorway is in the inner re-entrant of the south-west tower, with an empty panel-space above. An excellent wide turnpike stair with five-feet treads rises in this tower to the first floor. The basement contains two vaulted cellars, and the kitchen at the east end, with an enormous fireplace arch. A larder adjoins.

The Hall, on the first floor has been a fine chamber 35 by 18 feet, with private room off and laird's bedroom in the north-east tower. There has been much bedroom accommodation above, now inaccessible. The entire commodious house shows a high degree of workmanship.

The lands were granted by Bruce to Isabella Douglas, probably daughter of the Good Sir James, who married Walter de Oliphant, Justiciar of Scotland. Hatton passed to Halyburton of Pitcur in 1627, and then to the son of the notorious Mackenzie of Rosehaugh. It was garrisoned for the Covenant by the Earl of Crawford in 1645.

INVERGOWRIE HOUSE

A much altered fortalice of the late 16th and early 17th centuries, greatly enlarged in 1836, Invergowrie now stands surrounded by the modern outskirts of Dundee, near the Perthshire border, overlooking the Tay. Although it is difficult to trace the original work consistently, the early plan seems to have been a lengthy oblong, lying approximately north and south, the walls, roughcast, rising to three storeys. An angle-turret crowns the south-west corner, and a stair-turret corbelled out from first-floor level, rises to the north-east. The doorway, now built-up, lay just below this turret, from which it was defended by a shot-hole. The angle-turret is also provided with shot-holes. Nearly all the windows have been enlarged, and the present range of dormers is modern; but four pediments of the original dormers are built into the modern porch to the north, displaying variously the arms of Gray impaling Napier, the initials P.G. for Patrick Gray, and A.N. for Agnes Napier, the mottoes TRUST IN GOD and SOLI DE GRATIA, and the date 1601. The name AGNES NEPER also appears.

Internally the building has been greatly altered, and is now split up into flats. The basement is still vaulted, however, and the old kitchen is at the extreme south end of the range, being the basement chamber farthest from the door, as usual.

Invergowrie early belonged to the Abbey of Scone, and at the Reformation period passed to Sir John Carnegie of that Ilk. From him Sir Patrick Gray, brother of the 5th Lord Gray and uncle of the notorious Master of Gray, acquired the property in 1568, and built the house. The lands were forfeited after the Gowrie Conspiracy, and bestowed by James the Sixth on David Murray, first Viscount Stormont, one of the King's abettors in that murky

business. In 1615 however, they were bought by Robert Clayhills of Baldovie, of an eminent civic family in Dundee. A succession of Clayhills lairds retained Invergowrie, passing eventually by heiress to the Clayhill-Hendersons, in recent times.

INVERMARK CASTLE

At first glance Invermark seems to be a simple, typical tower of the late 16th or early 17th century. Closer inspection however reveals it to belong to two periods. Now four storeys and a garret in height, only the first three storeys belong to the early 16th century, when the tower was finished with a corbelled parapet and walk, the stumps of the supporting corbels still being visible. The upper storeys and the two-storeyed angle-turret were added a century later. Interesting features are the rounded corners of the walling and the two tall chimney-stacks to north and south which are pierced by window openings for the garret storey—most unusual.

The entrance is at first-floor level by an arched doorway still retaining its iron yett. It would be reached by the usual removable timber ladder or bridge. Sharing this level was the Hall and a smaller chamber. From the former a private stair gave the only access to the vaulted basement below, which was lit only by wide splayed gunloops. The upper floors were also subdivided.

Invermark stands in a strong strategic position at the head of Glen Esk, at the end of Loch Lee, and served as an outpost for the

larger castle of Edzell. It belonged to the Lindsays of Crawford and was useful for controlling the Highland caterans. David Lindsay 9th Earl of Crawford died here in 1558, and in 1607 Invermark became the hidingplace of Lord Edzell's son, another David, involved in the slaughter of Lord Spynie in Edinburgh.

INVERQUHARITY CASTLE

This fine old stronghold of the Ogilvys was once a place of major strength. It stands on the edge of the Carity Burn four miles northeast of Kirriemuir in what is now pastureland, and though no longer occupied it is fairly complete. Yet its present appearance is misleading, for it looks to be a typical and substantial oblong tower of the 15th century, whereas originally it was an L-planned building the east wing of which has completely disappeared, reputedly having been demolished to provide masonry for a farmsteading. Fortunately this cannibalism did not go beyond the wing, and the remainder retains numerous interesting and attractive features.

The walls, of good ashlar, reach eight feet in thickness, and rise four storeys to a parapet and walk, within which is the usual attic storey. The turnpike stair which now rises in the centre of the east front, previously, of course, rose in the usual place within the re-entrant angle with the missing wing. It terminates in a large caphouse, unusual in that the crowsteps of its small gables are themselves finished with tiny gablets—a feature seldom seen in secular buildings. The doorway, adjoining the stairway on the east front, has a fine pointed arch, and high above it, at parapet level, is a machicolated projection from which missiles could be dropped. The parapet is carried on good corbelling, and is provided with open rounds at three of its angles—the fourth having linked with the missing wing. The stone-flagged walk is drained by the usual cannon-like spouts.

The castle is somewhat unusual in containing two vaulted floors. The basement vault has had an intermediate timber floor, carried on corbels at the springing—quite a common method of increasing accommodation for servants. These floors are feebly lit by narrow slits. The Hall on the first floor is also vaulted, a handsome, high apartment. Normally the Hall is entered directly from the stairway, but in this case an elaborate arrangement has been contrived—presumably for security reasons—whereby, after leaving the main stair, a dog-legged ascent in the thickness of the walling rises up two sides of the building until the Hall door is reached. Another curious feature here is a sort of stone porch projecting into the north-west corner of the Hall, from which a few steps down in the thickness of the wall end at a window at a lower level. The reason for this escapes me. There is a handsome arched and moulded fireplace, two arched windows with stone seats, and a dark wall-chamber. Above have been bedrooms, each with fireplace and aumbry.

The iron yett or grille which guarded the entrance is interesting because the wording of the licence for its erection has been recorded—plus the fact that such licence was necessary. Granted by James Second in 1444, it says—'Rex—A licence be the King to Al. Ogilvy of Inercarity to fortify his house and put ane iron yet therein.' A second licence dating from 130 years later, shows that the need was still there—and that the royal scribes' spelling had deteriorated. 'Licence . . . gevin and grauntit full fredome faculty and spele to oure loud familiere squir Alex of Ogilvy of Inercarity for to fortifie his house and to strength it with an Irne yhet'. A serious business it must have been to put in an iron gate, when the King himself had to make such stipulations regarding it.

Sir John Ogilvy, third son of Walter Ogilvy of Auchterhouse, gained Inverquharity in 1420. One of his descendants, Alexander, was captured at Philiphaugh, fighting for Montrose, and was beheaded at Glasgow. Another fought for the dethroned King James at the Battle of the Boyne in Ireland. Fighting would come naturally to the Inverquharity lairds, for this district was soaked in blood from the eternal feuding between the Ogilvys and the Lindsays. This family received a baronetcy of Nova Scotia in 1626. The fifth baronet sold the property after it had been held for fourteen generations.

KELLY CASTLE

Kelly, not to be confused with Kellie Castle in Fife, is one of the finest and least altered examples of fortified laird's house in all Angus, and at first sight one of the best preserved. It was, nevertheless, in a ruinous state until restored a century ago. Happily, the restorers, of the Maule-Ramsay family, were content to do just that, rather than to 'improve' and extend, so that the entire house now gives little impression of alteration from its early state.

Standing on an eminence in the wooded glen of the Elliot Water, two miles west of Arbroath, it is often said to have been built by Sir William Irvine of the Drum family, but it seems more likely that he merely extended an earlier fortalice, for he acquired Kelly in 1614 and much of the building appears to be of earlier date. It consists of a tall five-storeyed tower on the L-plan, forming one corner of a courtyard, with lower buildings making up

[134]

the remaining sides, access being gained through a pend with gatehouse. Protecting this entrance is a flanking circular tower, at one corner, of no great height, with gunloops. Other shot-holes appear elsewhere.

The massive L-shaped tower, of red coursed rubble, with high steep roofs and crowstepped gables, has its main block enhanced by two turrets. That nearest the courtyard is a typical conical-roofed circular angle-turret, with shot-holes; but the other, crowning the opposite main corner of the building is unusual, being rectangular, three storeys in height with the two upper storeys rising above the general roof-level, the topmost forming a tiny gabled watch-chamber reached by a little turnpike stair corbelled out in a slender turret to one side. Nearby, above the main gable, rises a massive chimney-stack. The entire composition is an attractive amalgam of grace and strength. The windows throughout are notably regularly-placed and fair-sized, with moulded surrounds.

The doorway is in the re-entrant, within the courtyard. Nearby are three empty panel-spaces. Internally the house lives up to its outward appearance. The ground floor is vaulted. The Hall, on the first floor of the main block, is a fine room, pine-panelled.

The barony of Kelly, set up in early times for the family of Moubray, passed to a Stewart supporter of Bruce, and remained with his descendants until 1402 when it was acquired by the Ochterlonys—who indeed changed the property's name to Ochterlony, and thus it was known for two centuries. Although there is some question about continuing Ochterlony ownership through-out this period, there seems no doubt that Sir William Ochterlony sold Kelly in 1614 to Sir William Irvine above-mentioned, who presumably extended the house to the present form. It was ac-quired in 1679 by the third Earl of Panmure for £11,000 Scots on account of debts contracted by the Irvine laird on the King's behalf during the Civil War, and given to Harry Maule, the Earl's son, Deputy Lord Lyon King of Arms. He became one of the principal and most effective leaders in the Jacobite Rising of 1715, headed by his unpopular brother-in-law, Bobbing John, Earl of Mar. Kelly consequently became the scene of many exciting meet-ings and councils. His elder brother James, who had succeeded as 4th Earl of Panmure, was severely wounded and taken prisoner on the battlefield of Sheriffmuir but was gallantly rescued by Harry. At the collapse of the Rising, both brothers were outlawed but escaped by sea from nearby Arbroath, the Earl going to France but Harry Maule eventually settling in Holland. Neither

ever returned to Scotland. The title was attained and the estates forfeited, but eventually an Irish barony was created for Harry Maule's second son, as heir of the Panmures, and Kelly bought back. This title finally merged with the Maule-Ramsay Earldom of Dalhousie, and with that family Kelly still remains.

LOGIE HOUSE

Situated on level ground on an estate in Strathmore about two miles south of Kirriemuir, Logie is a tall plain tower-house of the 16th century which has been much altered two centuries later, the roof-line especially having suffered. It is oblong on plan with a circular stair-tower projecting at the north-east angle, now truncated and finishing with a flat oversailing roof. Much modern work has been added to the north, and built into a yard wall here is a former dormer pediment dated 1688. The main tower has been extended westwards also in the 18th century, and the west gable, with its elaborate finish, has a window lintel with the date 1022 and another with the initials D.K. and others that are weatherworn. The date is presumably a mistaken re-cutting. The walling throughout is harled and devoid of decoration. There is a shot-hole at third-floor level in the stair-tower.

[136]

Internally there has been much alteration, but the basement still contains a vaulted passage giving access to two vaulted chambers, one of which was the kitchen. There is a good wide turnpike stair. The Hall on the first floor has been subdivided. The house is in excellent condition, and there is some good 18th-century panelling.

Logie used to belong to a branch of the Wishart family. Indeed for long the estate was called Logie-Wishart. One 17th-century member was a royalist clergyman who became chaplain to the great Montrose, then Rector of Newcastle, and finally Bishop of Edinburgh. Later the lands passed to the Kinlochs of Kilrie.

MAINS CASTLE

It is unfortunate that so unusual and attractive an example of the 16th-century fortalice, and one so readily accessible to the people of Dundee, should have been allowed to sink into such a state of disrepair and neglect. Standing on the edge of a steep bank above a burn in Strathdichty, only three miles from the centre of the city, the building obviously belongs to various periods, but in the main it is a 16th-century house, constructed to form three sides of a courtyard, the fourth and west side being a high parapeted wall, now somewhat altered. This curtain-wall contains at its centre a good entrance gateway, arched and moulded, and surmounted by a massive corbelled projection or machicolated bar-

tizan, from which the usual missiles, boiling oil or water, could be dropped upon unwelcome guests. There are also shot-holes in the parapet crenellations—an unusual feature—and a long socket for a great oaken beam to strengthen the door. The keystone of the gateway arch is said formerly to have borne the date 1562 and the initials D.G. and D.M.O., for Sir David Graham and Dame Margaret Ogilvy his wife, daughter of a Lord Ogilvy of Airlie.

The main buildings lay on the north side of the square, and out of this rises the notably lofty and unusual stair-tower. This is so high as to be almost out of proportion. The ground to the south, however, rises rapidly, and this was probably necessary to give a field of view for the watch-chamber at the top. The tower reaches six storeys, and although the corbelling of the top storey is original, the rather peculiar finish to the four gablets is certainly of later date. These gablets are not crowstepped in the usual way.

The entrance was in the foot of this stair-tower, in which the turnpike rises. The basement contained vaulted cellars and stores. The Hall would be on the first floor, with domestic accommodation above, but this side of the courtyard is now in a delapidated condition.

The eastern range seems to be of slightly later date, and in somewhat better state. At its south end is a doorway with early Renaissance decoration, and the remarkable inscription PATRIAE ET POSTERIS GRATIS ET AMICIS, which could mean Grateful for Country, for Friends and for Posterity. The south range has almost entirely disappeared, and was no doubt servants' accommodation. Traces of a bakehouse survive.

In the 14th century the property belonged to the Earls of Angus, but it is as a Graham house that Mains is known. John Graham of Balargus, a cadet of the Grahams of Fintry in Stirlingshire, acquired the Claverhouse estate in 1530. It was almost certainly his son, Sir David, who built Mains as it now stands, though there may well have been some earlier building there. He changed the property's name to Fintry, after the family's ancestral home in the west. This laird was a nephew of the murdered Cardinal Beaton—though he is on record as having forgiven the murderers of his distinctly unpopular uncle thirty years later. He was involved in the shady affairs of the 'Spanish Blanks', whereby Huntly and other Catholic nobles sent blank letters, fully signed to the King of Spain, for him to fill in his own terms for aiding them in restoring the Romish faith to Scotland, in 1592. Sir David was beheaded in consequence. Thereafter the Grahams of Fintry (or Mains) wisely seem to have kept out of the history-books—unlike their cousin of Claverhouse.

MELGUND CASTLE

This is one of the most interesting and impressive castles in Angus, architecturally, despite being a roofless ruin. It stands on high ground, above the steep bank of a burn, one mile east of Aberlemno. At first glance it seems to be a typical 15th-century keep, with large extensions of the 16th century, as at Edzell etc.; but closer inspection reveals that all the building is of a piece and period, dating from the mid-16th century. This is in fact a copy of earlier castles that have developed in this fashion—with improvements. The keep is L-planned, the six-feet thick walls of good coursed red sandstone rubble rising four storeys to an elaborate corbel-table which supports a parapet-walk provided with open rounds at all angles. The stair-wing (to the left of sketch) has been carried higher to form a large watch-chamber, rather than the usual small caphouse. All above the parapet is ruinous, but there would be the usual garret storey within the walk. The windows

are small, and the walls well provided with wide splayed gunloops.

The entrance, at the far side of the stair-wing, admits to the wide turnpike stair and to the two vaulted cellars of the keep. In an earlier castle, the first floor apartment would have been the Hall; but here the extension built at the same time has provided space for a larger Hall, and the keep first floor contains only a private room. This has windows with stone seats, a smallish fireplace in a corner, and mural recesses from which gunloops open. There is a peculiar garderobe with inner dark recess off it, which might have been used as a prison. The upper floors contained bedroom accommodation.

The extension to the east is most interesting. It is only two storeys and an attic in height, but along its south side it has also been provided with a parapet and walk, on similar ornamental corbelling. At the north-east angle is a round tower with shot-holes. There has been a range of secondary building along the north face, now completely ruinous, which has had a vaulted passage below and three small bedrooms above. In the main extension the vaulted basement contained the kitchen to the west, with a huge arched fireplace in the keep walling, and four cellars to the east. A secondary turnpike rises beside the round tower. Above was the Hall, a magnificent apartment, with a great handsome fireplace in the north wall, the massive chimney for which can be seen in sketch. A narrow private stair leads down to the wine-cellar below. A withdrawing-room opened eastwards of the Hall, and there were attic bedrooms above.

Melgund was built by the famous Cardinal Beaton, Archbishop

of St. Andrews and Chancellor of Scotland. Jervise declared that his initials D.B. and those of his mistress and 'chief lewd' Marion Ogilvy, appear over certain windows. These I could not see. There is a theory that Beaton was in fact early married to Marion, daughter of the 1st Lord Ogilvy of Airlie, but that when he decided to pursue his ambitions through the priesthood, he demoted her to the status of mistress, having to legitimate his sons thereafter. Though some have questioned his building of this castle, it certainly would seem to be the work of a man of great vision and ambition. The Beaton ownership ended in the 17th century, when Melgund passed to the Marquis of Huntly. The Marquis, summoned to Edinburgh to answer a charge of treason, was stormbound here one winter, and eventually carried as far as Dundee 'in ane coache, borne upone long treis upone menis arms, becauss horss micht not trauell in respect of the gryt storme and deipness of the way clad with snaw and frost'. Melgund passed to the Maules and then the Murrays, and thence by an heiress to the Earl of Minto, whose son still bears the title of Viscount Melgund.

MURROES CASTLE

Standing in an attractive garden in the pleasant hamlet of Murroes, near the church, three miles north of Broughty Ferry, this is a small fortalice of the late 16th century. At one time a bothy for farm workers, it has been lovingly restored.

There is a long narrow main block of two storeys, lying north and south, with a circular stair-tower projecting centrally to the west. The walls are well supplied with shot-holes and gunloops, and the original windows have moulded surrounds. The internal arrangements are difficult to describe owing to irregular floor levels caused by the sloping site. Thus the entrance is at first-floor level on the east, reached by a modern forestair—no doubt formerly of timber and removable—but this is ground level at the west (as seen in sketch). Similarly the stair-tower rises from ground level on the west, but internally is supported on massive corbels five feet above the kitchen floor—a unique arrangement in my experience. There is no vaulting.

The door gives access to the kitchen, probably formerly the Hall, subdivided in modern times to give an additional lobby and small bedroom. Steps lead down, into a dark semi-subterranean chamber. The tower stair rises to a pleasant panelled room above, and higher to a range of intercommunicating bedrooms.

[141]

The Fotheringhams of Fotheringham, Tealing, Powrie and
Murroes, were a powerful Angus family from early times, first
appearing in the 14th century. Murroes has much in common with
nearby Powrie, and much of the panelling came from demolished
Fotheringham House.

PITCUR CASTLE

This massive and rather strange-looking castle stands close to the
main road between Dundee and Coupar Angus, about three miles
south-east of the latter, amongst the Sidlaw Hills. It is a substan-
tially-built structure, apparently of the 16th century, now ruinous
but maintained in good condition. Farmhouse and steading adjoin.
Unfortunately the roofline has been altered and finished-off in an
extraordinary fashion, much detracting from the appearance of
the building.

The castle now conforms to the T-plan, with main block lying
east and west and a wing projecting centrally northwards, while
a circular stair-tower rises in the north-west re-entrant. This
northern wing, however, appears to be an addition to the earlier
oblong. The well-built walls, of good red-brown coursed rubble,
rise to four storeys, and no doubt formerly ended in an attic storey
above. The windows are mainly small, the stair-tower is ringed by
stringcourses, and the arched and moulded doorway in the north
front of the wing is still provided with a good iron yett. Above is
an empty panel-space, with dripstone and spout.

The main block retains two vaulted chambers, but the vault of
the kitchen, which has occupied the basement of the wing, has
fallen in. The Hall above, in the main block, appears to have been

a fine apartment. This, with sleeping accommodation higher, is now inaccessible.

At an early date this property belonged to a branch of the Chisholm family. In 1432 Walter, second son of the 1st Lord Halyburton of Dirleton married the co-heiress of Alexander de Chisholm, and thus obtained Pitcur. The Halyburtons remained long in possession, becoming chief representers of that name.

PITKERRO CASTLE

Pitkerro is a small fortalice of the late 16th century to which a large modern mansion has been grafted, set in wooded policies two miles north of Broughty Ferry. The original work consists of a long and narrow main block of two storeys, with a circular stair-tower projecting on the east front, rising a storey higher, and corbelled out to the square at top to form the usual watch-chamber. This is reached by a little stair-turret in the re-entrant, supported on a tiny squinch or crosswise arch. The angle-turret crowning the south-west gable is a renewal. The old house was drastically altered during the 19th century, turrets removed and the roof pitch lowered. In 1902 Sir Robert Lorimer restored the building with his usual good taste, giving the turrets the ogee roofs to which he was so partial. The dormer pediments are also reconstructions, as is the crowstepping of the gables. The walls are roughcast.

The original door is in the foot of the stair-tower, surmounted by a panel dated 1593 and the initials I.D. and I.F. The basement

is not vaulted and contains the old kitchen and three cellars. Above was the Hall, with private rooms adjoining.

By 1534 Pitkerro was possessed by John Durham, second son of Durham of Grange of Monifeith, but the builder would seem to have been his son James. His grandson, Sir James, was knighted by Charles First, and he was succeeded by another Sir James, Clerk of the Exchequer. *His* son, Sir Alexander Durham, was a soldier, colonel of his own regiment in the Civil Wars and Lord Lyon King of Arms. The lands were later sold to the Dick family.

POWRIE CASTLE

Standing on high ground three miles north of Dundee, Powrie Castle could be said to be in reduced circumstances. Its early massive keep is a complete ruin, and its 17th-century range occupied by farm workers. These are two distinct buildings, formerly linked together by an enclosing curtain-wall and courtyard. The keep dates probably from the late 15th century, but little of it remains.

The northern range, as seen in sketch, is a long two-storeyed building of the early 17th century, added at a time when lairds and their ladies were demanding more comfort and convenience in their living quarters. It is of excellent workmanship, showing Renaissance features, notably in its carved and pilastered windows. It consists of a main block measuring 73 by 20 feet, with a round tower at the north-west corner. This does not contain a turnpike stair, as is usual, but has a large vaulted oven in the basement, and a private chamber off the laird's room above—a comfortably warm neuk on occasion. There is an attractive two-storeyed porch near the centre of the south front, with fine ornamental windows, over one of which is the date 1604. On the upper floor of this porch was the entrance doorway, reached either by a removable timber stair or a wooden gallery. The wide turnpike stairway is just within this door, projecting into the accommodation, and leading down to the basement.

This ground floor has a vaulted bakery at the west end, from which the aforementioned oven opens, with its own doorway. There is a kitchen at the east end, with a huge fireplace occupying all the gable-end. The kitchen has no connection with the upper floor, which must have been inconvenient. It seems obvious that this entire range was added only as a domestic complement to the larger and now ruinous keep. There are two smaller chambers on the ground floor, and three large and two small apartments above, arranged in two suites, now reached by a modern wooden stair. The building is highly unusual in having no fewer than six other doors on the south side, one now built up; but this insecure arrangement is accounted for by the fact that the entire building itself stood within the powerful enclosing walls of the old castle. None of the doorways face outwards.

Wester Powrie, as it was formerly called, was granted by William the Lion to the Laird of Ogilvy about 1170 and remained with that family until acquired by Thomas Fotheringham in 1412. This family, said to have been originally of Hungarian extraction, provided a number of members of the old Scottish parliament. In 1666 David Fotheringham of Powrie bought from Patrick, 7th Lord Gray, the Castle of Broughty. Alexander of Powrie fought for the Jacobites at Sheriffmuir in 1715 and was captured, but later escaped in Edinburgh. This escape is described in a letter, dated 3rd June 1716, from the Countess of Panmure to her husband, who had been Fotheringham's commanding officer. 'Last week Poorie made his escape from his Lodgings in ye Cannongate, having gott liberty to come out of my Lord Winton's house to take a course of Physick; so he had onlie sentries on him. . . .' The castle was destroyed by the Scrymgeours of Dudhope in 1492, and the present older building was probably erected thereafter on the same site. This itself was damaged in 1547, when the invading English were garrisoning Broughty Castle and 'became exceedingly insolent and spoiled and burnt the country at

[145]

their pleasure, and among the rest the town of Dundee and the Castle of Wester Powrie with the village adjacent', according to Pitscottie, who apparently evaluated Dundee and Powrie Castle more or less equally. That same year, the laird, another Thomas Fotheringham, fell at the Battle of Pinkie. It was still another Thomas who built the northern range, and who married in 1593 Barbara, daughter of Sir Walter Scott of Balamy.

Yet another Thomas Fotheringham petitioned the King, in 1737, to grant him a pardon for 'the unpremeditated murder of Dennis Wright, or McIntyre', at Florence. He averred that they 'were heated with drink' at the time, and began by 'throwing Bottles and glasses'. Later, he adds, 'Your Petitioner having unluckily got into his hand a Hanger (sword) that was lying in the Room, I gave the said Dennis a wound in the Belly.' The unfortunate Dennis died two days later, absolving Fotheringham from 'all prosecutions that may arise on account of this accident'. Whether pardon was granted is not recorded.

KINCARDINESHIRE

ALLARDYCE CASTLE

Set picturesquely on a terrace in a bend of the deep valley of the Bervie Water, about two miles west of Inverbervie, Allardyce is an interesting and attractive mansion of probably the late 16th century now occupied as a farmhouuse. Although giving the impression of belonging all to one period, the two wings of its original L-plan have in fact been extended, that to the west very considerably, about a century later. The building has formed two sides of a courtyard, the remainder of which has been enclosed by a curtain-wall, and access thereto gained by an attractive pend slapped through the basement of the main block—a fairly unusual arrangement. Also highly unusual is the amount and great intricacy of the label corbelling supporting the stair-turret which rises in the re-entrant angle. This is corbelled out at the top to form a gabled watch-chamber, reached by a secondary turret stair and flanked by a slender angle-turret, the entire composition being most pleasing. Other notable features are the off-setting of the walling to the west, and the tall chimney-stack rising above this front. In the main the walls rise to four storeys and an attic, and are roughcast and whitewashed. The basement is vaulted, and the usual arrangement of kitchen premises below, Hall on first floor and sleeping accommodation above, would apply. A stone built into part of the extension is dated 1695.

The name Allardyce has had more than the usual variations in spelling. We read that Alesaundre de Abberdash and Walterus de Allerdas signed the notorious Ragman Roll of English Edward the First at the end of the 13th century. Shortly afterwards Robert Bruce gave a charter of the property under the name of Alrethes to one Duncan Judicii. This Duncan and his descendants adopted the name of Allardyce of that Ilk for themselves, and retained possession for many centuries. In 1656 however spelling difficult-

[147]

ies were still cropping up, for Cromwell, nominating justices for the county of Kincardine, included one Thomas Ardes, Tutor of the same. In 1662 Sir John Allardyce married the Lady Mary Graham, grand-daughter of the unfortunate Earl of Airth. At the turn of the 18th century, however, the Allardyce heiress carried the property to her husband, Barclay of Urie in the same county. The famous pedestrian, Captain Barclay-Allardyce, was notable for his long-distance walking. He died in 1854, and with him it seems the long line of Allardyce of Allardyce became extinct.

BALBEGNO CASTLE

This highly interesting and attractive 16th-century house stands half-a-mile south-west of Fettercairn, the ancient portion being practically unused whilst the modern extension is occupied as a farmhouse. It corresponds to the L-plan, although its architectural history is not quite as appears at first glance. It looks like a tall L-shaped tower-house of the mid-16th century, with a plain gabled 17th-century extension to west and later, lower work to east and in the re-entrant angle; however, McGibbon and Ross, who made a careful study, were satisfied that only the upper storey of the western portion is a reconstruction and that otherwise this was all an integral part of the original building, the parapet and walk which now crowns the east side of the wing having previously continued right round the house at this level, traces of it remaining at the eastern gabling.

[148]

The main house is four storeys and a garret in height, the walls being roughcast, and the parapet of ashlar with ornamental medallion heads. The stair-wing of the L rises somewhat higher, to finish in an elaborately decorated watch-chamber, provided with an angle-turret with oversailing roof—this having formerly been one of the open rounds of the parapet. The watch-chamber, reached by a turret stair corbelled out in the re-entrant, is enhanced with heraldic panels and carved work, inscribed I.WOD and E.IRVEIN and ANO 1569. The house is well provided with splayed gunloops and circular shot-holes.

Although unfortunately the re-entrant angle at ground level has been filled in by a modern porch, masking the original entrance, this was in the usual position at the foot of the stair-wing. The basement is vaulted, and contained the old kitchen and cellars. The Hall on the first floor is most interesting, having a very fine groined and ribbed vaulted ceiling, painted in tempera with heraldic devices of some of the principal families of Scotland, including Wood and Irvine. There is a private room at this level in the wing. Above, the second floor is divided into four bedchambers, each with garderobe. Higher is further domestic accommodation.

Balbegno was granted to Andrew Wood of Over Blairton by James Fourth in 1488, of the family which had been hereditary constables of the royal castle of Kincardine. His son John succeeded in 1512 and married Elizabeth Irvine of Drum, building

the present castle. Five generations of Woods followed, and then Balbegno was sold in 1687 to Andrew Middleton, youngest brother of the notorious Earl of Middleton. Later it passed to the Ogilvies, who added the more modern work.

In 1596 Catherine, a widow, complained to the Privy Council that William Wood, brother of the laird, stole from her twelve sheep and three kye so that she is 'compelled to beg for misery and lack of food'. At her first complaint, to the Sheriff of Kincardine, 'Wode put violent hands on her, dang and strack her and said gyf he ever found her plainting on him he should cast her in a peat pot and drown her'. King James Sixth put Wood in Brechin Tolbooth until the lady's goods were restored. William was in trouble again in 1601 when the laird had to find 10,000 merks caution to enter him in ward at Edinburgh Castle. They seem to have been an unruly family, for in 1624 David Wood, uncle of Sir John of Balbegno, was ordered on pain of 500 merks not to molest William Wishart, minister of Fettercairn. The last Wood laird was a companion-in-arms of the royalist Earl Middleton. It was agreed that if one fell in battle he would endeavour to come back and describe the other world. Balbegno fell, and duly appeared to Middleton, prisoner in the Tower of London. He foretold Middleton's rise to fame, apparently, but his description of the hereafter lacks precision:

'Plumashes above, Gramashes below,
It's no wonder to see how the world doth go.'

BENHOLM TOWER

This tall and imposing castle, though now ruinous, stands impressively above a deep ravine overlooking the sea two miles south-west of Inverbervie. Attached is a more modern mansion, now much more delapidated than the stout old tower itself.

Square on plan, the 15th-century keep rises four storeys and eighty feet to a crenellated parapet borne on simple individual corbels, having open rounds at the angles. Above has been a garret storey. At the south-east angle the stairway ends in a square gabled caphouse and watch-chamber of somewhat later date, which fills one of the open rounds. The thick-walled masonry is massive red coursed rubble.

A door in the south front admits to the two basement vaults. The Hall on the first floor is large, provided with deep wall-

chambers, and a good ornamental aumbry near the great fireplace. The windows have stone seats, and one still retains its iron yett. The upper floors, now inaccessible, were probably subdivided.

Benholm was a seat of the Keiths, near kin to the Earls Marischal of nearby Dunnottar Castle, though said to have been built by an Ogilvie. In 1565 the Privy Council appointed its laird as keeper of the haven of Bervie, In 1618 James Keith of Benholm, with his father George, Earl Marischal, had to find caution to the Council for inciting Andro Barclay and others to assault Robert Falconer 'which they accordingly did'. Five years later Benholm was the scene of the theft of much money and jewellery by the Earl's widowed Countess.

CRATHES CASTLE

One of the most famous and handsome castles in Scotland, Crathes, the ancient home of the Burnett of Leys family, stands in a large estate on the north bank of the Dee, three miles east of Banchory, in that enclave of Kincardineshire which thrusts north into Aberdeenshire. One of the group of magnificent houses which includes Midmar, Craigievar and Castle Fraser, it is a lofty but massive tower of the 16th century, basically square on plan but with a small projecting wing, to which later work has been

attached. It is built of a warm-toned granite, with the angles rounded, and rises to four storeys and an attic. The lower storeys are very plain, but above first-floor level the exterior breaks out in a flourish of corbelling, stringcourses, angle- and stair-turrets, heraldic decoration, gargoyles, gabling, and similar features, which are the unique glory of Scottish castellated architecture, and which here reaches its fullest flowering. Externally, of particular interest are the squared and gabled turrets, almost watch-chambers, which alternate with the normal circular angle-turrets at eaves-level; the fashion in which a stair-turret is squared off to form a clock-tower and crenellated look-out platform; and the machicolated projection-cum-dormer window sited high above the doorway in the re-entrant angle, for the down-casting of missiles upon unwelcome guests. The large modern window opened at first-floor level, as seen in sketch, only slightly detracts from the authentic appearance.

Internally Crathes is as fine as its outer aspect, its plaster and tempera ceilings being famous, as is the woodwork of its top-floor gallery and many other features. But all has been described times without number and there is no need for elaboration here. One of its precious relics, the jewelled ivory Horn of Leys, is said to have been presented by King Robert the Bruce to Alexander de Burnard or Burnett when he received his charter of the lands in 1323.

The family, like Irvine of Drum nearby, have one of the longest continuous tenures of occupation in the land, and took a prominent part in much of Scottish history. Robert Burnett was the Baron o' Leys of the ancient 15th-century ballad, and Thomas Burnett, twelfth Laird of Leys and uncle of the famous Bishop Gilbert Burnett, was created a Baronet of Nova Scotia in 1626. The Leys referred to was a small loch and its surroundings situated a couple of miles to the west. Muchalls Castle, near Stonehaven, was also a seat of this family, which they acquired shortly before 1619, when Archibald Burnett, father of the first Baronet, built much of the present work. He was also responsible for the crowning glories at Crathes.

Although the Burnett family still retain a connection, Crathes was handed over to the National Trust for Scotland, with an upkeep endowment, in 1951.

DUNNOTTAR CASTLE

This famous and magnificently sited stronghold of the great Earls Marischal, covers an area of nearly four acres on top of a lofty and isolated promontory of rock thrusting into the sea a mile and a half south of Stonehaven, all but severed from the mainland by a deep chasm. The strongly defensive position was the scene of many battles even during the Pictish period, and was the ancient capital of The Mearns. Nevertheless, the oldest buildings of which traces remain were ecclesiastical, not military, for curiously enough the parish church and graveyard were situated on this inconvenient rock when, in the 14th century, Sir William Keith, Great Marischal of Scotland built a stronghold there, removing the church. For this sacrilege he was excommunicated, but reinstated by the Pope on payment of recompense to the Church and building a new kirk in a more convenient position.

The present extensive remains date from various periods. The oldest portion is the tall and massive square early 15th-century keep, seen in sketch, L-planned, containing four main storeys beneath a parapet on fairly simple corbelling, with a now fragmentary garret storey above. The walls, of coursed rubble, are pierced by gunloops and there are open rounds at all angles. The basement is vaulted, and besides the usual cellars contains a small prison. There are two Halls, that on the first floor being the Common Hall, with the former kitchen alongside, having a large fire-

[153]

place, oven and sink. The Earl's or Upper Hall was on the second floor, better lighted, with private apartments higher.

The gatehouse is particularly interesting. Known as Benholm's Lodging, it is approached by a steep path and defended by no fewer than three tiers of wide splayed gunloops. The arched entrance gateway, 5½ feet wide, is the only opening in a solid wall of masonry 35 feet high, crowned with a parapet, wedged in a great cleft of the rock. Within was a portcullis and then a flight of steps, down which point four more oval gunloops.

The many extensions preclude any adequate description here. To the east were stables—the horses presumably trained to climb stairs!—retainers' barracks, and a priest's house and graveyard. The buildings to the north-west, grouped round a quadrangle and dating from the late 16th and early 17th centuries, included a chapel, a gallery 120 feet long, library, dining and withdrawing-rooms. There is a water cistern 20 feet in diameter, a forge for casting iron bullets, and a bowling-green.

Dunnottar's stirring history can only be hinted at here. Wallace captured it. Edward the Third did likewise and re-fortified it on his progress through Scotland—though it fell again to Sir Andrew Moray the Regent immediately afterwards. The 5th Earl Marischal, a noted scholar, traveller and founder of Marischal College, Aberdeen, erected most of the extensions. Montrose besieged Dunnottar, and failing to take it, burned much of the Marischal's surrounding property. In 1650 the 9th Earl entertained Charles the Second here, and the following year it was selected as the strongest place in the kingdom to deposit the Scottish regalia from

Cromwell's triumphant army. General Lambert besieged the castle, and the smuggling-out of the regalia, before starvation compelled surrender, is one of the best-known episodes of Scottish history. Dunnottar's name was thereafter stained by the immuring here of 167 Covenanters, men and women, in 1685, barbarously packed into a small vault at the hot season, wherein nine died. Twenty-five, in desperation, managed to get out and crawl along the sheer cliff, where two fell to their death. The others, re-captured, were subjected to terrible tortures.

The great family of the Earls Marischal is no more, and their castle now in the care of the Ministry of Works.

DURRIS HOUSE

On the south bank of Dee, at the northern extremity of the county and eight miles east of Banchory, Durris House stands in a large and ancient estate. The house, still occupied and cared for, is particularly interesting as being much other than it seems. At first glance it would appear to be a simple smallish oblong laird's house of the early 17th century, to which a larger mansion has been attached in later times. Actually what remains probably represents portions of a large courtyard-type castle of an earlier date, much of the vaulted basement foundations of which survive below present ground level.

The tower is not even oblong, as it now appears, but L-planned, comprising a main block and taller stair-wing, which culminates in a little watch-chamber slightly built out on a series of simple individual corbels. The re-entrant angle of the L has been filled in with later work, probably in the 17th century, and the roof-level somewhat altered, the yellow-washed harling now covering the traces of this addition. It is possible that the tower originally finished in a parapet with walk, and the two very small and unusual angle-turrets at the western corners might represent the former open rounds for this; in which case the squared watch-chamber would have served as a caphouse—as at Darnick Tower, Roxburghshire, a fortalice which Durris much resembles externally.

The two doors in the present south gable are of course modern, the original entrance being now internal, in the foot of the stair-wing, as was normal. The present ground-floor chamber is not vaulted, but there is a vaulted basement below this level. Whether the entire ground level has been altered, or whether these basements were always subterranean, remains to be settled. The strong

position on the edge of the steep bank of a stream could have facilitated a terracing operation. The ceiling of the ground-floor chamber has been raised, the corbels for the former joists still projecting. The Hall is on the first floor above, and is unusual in that it contains two fireplaces, despite its comparatively modest dimensions—a large one near the door, and a smaller one opposite. The room seems rather too small for one of these to have been used for cooking purposes, divided from the rest by a timber screen, as was frequently the arrangement. There are bedrooms higher, and on each floor there is a small chamber in the filled-in re-entrant angle. A tiny turnpike stair without external projection, admits to the watch-chamber at the main stairhead. This little room has an unusual stone seat at one side of one of its small windows.

There has been much modern addition to north and east, but directly across from the old tower, at the eastern extremity, there is a tall squared building which might represent at least the base of a former courtyard flanking-tower. It has another subterranean vaulted basement, from which other vaults extend below the present modern house. Altogether the house confronts the viewer with a fascinating puzzle.

The Durris estate, which used to compromise almost the entire parish, was held from the 13th century by a branch of the great family of Fraser. It passed by marriage of the heiress to the famous Charles Mordaunt, Earl of Peterborough, towards the end of the 17th century. Their daughter married in 1706 the 2nd Duke of Gordon, and the 4th Duke eventually heired Durris. The property was sold in 1834 to Anthony Mactier, formerly of Calcutta, who made enlargements, and sold again, for no less than £300,000 in 1871. The house was burned by Montrose at the same time as was Castle Fraser, the Frasers being strong Covenanters.

FIDDES CASTLE

This is a delightful and interesting example of a moderately sized fortalice of the second half of the 16th century, still occupied and in excellent condition, standing on open high ground four miles south-west of Stonehaven on the north side of Bruxie Hill. There was a charter of Queen Mary, dated 1553, of the lands of Fiddes in favour of Andrew Arbuthnot, second son of Arbuthnot of that Ilk, whose house of that name stands about five miles to the south.

The building follows a modification of the L-plan, with main block lying north and south and a wing extending to the east. A large circular stair-tower rises in the re-entrant and actually projects round beyond the gable of the main block—a most unusual feature. This tower has an open platform roof, which was at one time roofed over; its parapet is carried on individual corbelling, and there is a machicolated projection to defend the doorway beneath. Also unusual is another circular tower which rises at the south-west angle of the main block, the other corner of the same gable, which is thus notably narrowed. This is corbelled out to the square at the top, to form a small watch-chamber. A tall stair-turret projects approximately midway along the north front, at the junction of wing and main block, above first-floor level, and this is also corbelled out to the square at top. Two-storey angle-turrets crown the wing gable and also the north-west corner of the main block. A tiny stair-turret rises between main block south gable and main stair-tower. Altogether a most elaborate and interesting composition. The walls rise to three storeys and an attic, and are well supplied with the usual shot-holes. Notable are the tiny shot-holes opened in the continuous corbelling of the angle-turrets for downwards shooting. There is an empty panel space on the machicolated projection above the doorway, and the south-east dormer pediment has been renewed, bearing the date 1593.

The basement is vaulted, the kitchen to the east containing a large fireplace arch. From the adjoining chamber, no doubt the wine-cellar, a private stair rises to the Hall above. The main wide turnpike stair ascends only to the first floor, the ascent thereafter

being continued in the other round tower and in the northern stair-turret. The Hall occupies the first floor of the main block, and there is a private room in the wing, with a tiny chamber off it which has a finely decorative ceiling. There is ample bedroom accommodation above.

The founder of the Arbuthnots was a Borderer, of the family of Swinton of that Ilk, which is said to itself have derived from the princely Earls of Dunbar and March. Hugo de Swinton, probably having married the heiress, came north and took the name of Arbuthnot late in the 12th century. How early they owned Fiddes is uncertain, but we read that Sir Robert Arbuthnot of Arbuthnot, in favour with James Third and Fourth, recovered the lands of Fiddes which had been alienated for 200 years. In 1654 Andrew, second son of another Sir Robert Arbuthnot is designated as of Fiddes, having bought it from his cousin. He married Helen, daughter of Sir David Lindsay of Edzell, and is said to have 'died in the flower of his age of that disease his father died, and in likelihood had propagated to him'. He had however many children, and his second son, John, sold Fiddes to James Thomson of Arduthie.

The castle is now a farmhouse, restored and lovingly cared for.

GLENBERVIE HOUSE

The mansion of Glenbervie, in foothill country eight miles south-west of Stonehaven, compounds ancient and modern, with modern tending to dominate the aspect although most of the building is ancient. The work seen here belongs to three main periods; the two massive round towers have been the flanking-towers of a courtyard-type castle of early date, with some of the curtain-walling still traceable; the gable of a lofty later house of probably the 17th century, to the south; and the entire roof-line and northern frontage altered in pseudo-baronial style, with decorations, in modern times.

Some ancient features survive. There are wide splayed gun-loops in both towers, slit windows, and an iron yett in a basement window near the present front door. The basement is vaulted, and owing to the falling away of the ground level southwards, semi-subterranean.

Glenbervie Castle was a famous stronghold, held from the 12th century by the Melville family. Edward of England resided here in 1296, and John de Melville did homage. Another laird John, Sheriff of Kincardine was for his sins boiled in a cauldron on Hill of Garvock, by four local lairds, who supped of the broth and were thereafter outlawed for the crime. In 1468 a Melville heiress carried Glenbervie to Sir Alexander Auchinleck, whose own daughter brought it to Sir William Douglas, a son of the Earl of

Angus. So started a long succession of Douglas lairds, later baronets, one of who compiled the famous Douglas Peerage.

HALLGREEN CASTLE

Standing at the southern outskirts of Inverbervie, looking across Bervie Bay to the headland of Craig David, Hallgreen is an L-planned house of the late 16th century, with an earlier nucleus, to which a more modern mansion has been attached to north and west. The fronts to south and east are old work, although that to the east has been partially rebuilt. They show a fairly typical medium-sized laird's house, in local red-brown sandstone, of three storeys and an attic, with steep roofs, crowstepped gables, dormer windows, and corner-turrets at the angles left unaltered by later additions. There are wide splayed gunloops on these fronts, relics presumably of the earlier castle on the site, those to the east being of the double-aperture variety. Many windows have been enlarged and others built up. A peculiar buttress projects at the south-east angle, seemingly as a strengthening of the walling here, where the ground level drops away steeply to the ravine of a burn. The basement of the house is vaulted, and the usual arrangement of Hall on first floor and bedroom accommodation above would apply.

Hallgreen Castle is said to have been founded by the Dunnet family in 1376, but passed to the Raits in the 15th century—one

of whom was a Captain of the Guard to James the Fourth—which family would be responsible for most of the building now extant. The house is still in occupation.

INGLISMALDIE CASTLE

This fine, late 16th-century tower-house, although now only the nucleus of a large mansion of various periods, still dominates the rest by its height, vigorous lines and air of enduring strength. It stands near the North Esk, in the forested area six miles north-east of Brechin, at the very southern edge of the county. The original building is an L-planned fortalice of warm red coursed rubble, of three main storeys, an attic and a garret, with angle-turrets crowning the corners, and the unusual feature of a matching half-turret centred at the wallhead on the present front of the house (as seen in sketch). These turrets are supported on elaborate label-corbelling, and the label design is repeated in the unusual stringcourse which returns round the building at second-floor level. This has been copied on some of the later extensions. The roofs of the turrets are modern, and somewhat too steeply pointed; in McGibbon and Ross's sketch of 1892, the turrets are shown as truncated, with oversailing roofs, themselves not original.

The fine doorway in what is now the front, surmounted by a renewed heraldic panel and earl's coronet, is modern, the former entrance, which can still be traced internally, being on the west front, now enclosed by modern work. It was protected by twin shot-holes, as is the present south front at basement level.

The interior has necessarily been much altered and modernised, but much that is excellent remains. The exceedingly wide and handsome turnpike stair is a notable feature. The basement is vaulted, and the original Hall would be on the first floor, where the main stair ends, the ascent thereafter formerly being continued in a turret stair which no doubt projected in the re-entrant angle, now hidden amongst modern extensions. There is some excellent carved woodwork within. McGibbon and Ross's sketch shows a chapel, surmounted by a stone cross, to the east of the present front; this was later converted into kitchen premises. The name was originally Ecclesmaldie or Eglismaldie, referring to a cell dedicated to St. Maldie or Mallie.

After the Reformation, these church lands seem to have come into the possession of a branch of the Livingstone family. The King granted in 1588 a charter to John Livingstone of Dunipace

of various lands including Over, Middle and Nether Eglismaldie in Kincardine. The Livingstones were still there in 1631, but in 1635 the lands passed to Sir John Carnegie, Sheriff of Forfar, who, having been created 1st Earl of Ethie, later changed his title by royal consent, to Earl of Northesk and Baron Rosehill and Inglismaldie. In 1693, however, David Falconer of Newton, son of Sir David, Lord Newton, President of the College of Justice, obtained the property. By the death of his cousin he became 5th Lord Falconer of Halkerton, an old Mearns family descended from the royal falconers of Kincardine Castle. His sister married Joseph Home of Ninewells, and was the mother of David Home or Hume the philosopher. He himself married Lady Catherine Keith, eldest daughter of the 2nd Earl of Kintore in 1703, when she was thirteen. He died at Inglismaldie, 1751.

In 1778 Anthony, 8th Lord Falconer succeeded as 5th Earl of Kintore. He was exceedingly eccentric, having a great propensity for shooting his tenants' and neighbours' barndoor fowls. His fowling exploits included shooting a small bird which had flown in through an open window of Logie-Pert church, during service —which, he explained, was to prevent the bird disturbing the minister and congregation. Inglismaldie remained with this family until modern times, when it passed from their hands, to be bought again in 1925 by Major Adrian Keith-Falconer, a cousin of the Earl. He and his wife died in 1959 and since 1960 the castle has been in the appreciative possession of a member of the family of Ogilvie.

LAURISTON CASTLE

This strongly-sited fortalice, perched high above its deep wooded den, has fallen on evil days indeed. It has been a courtyard-type castle of various dates, to which a more modern mansion has been added. This is now only a gaunt shell, but two portions of the earlier work survive, linked by a fine section of the high curtain-wall which formerly enclosed the courtyard, complete with its parapet and walk—a feature which seldom survives. Of these two structures, that to the west is the older, apparently one of the original square flanking towers of the corners, seeming almost to grow out of the living rock of a shoulder of the ravine. Unfortunately it has been heightened in an unsightly fashion in modern times, but is authentic as far as parapet-level. A door opens from the courtyard, and the tower rises three storeys above this level, and sinks one below. The narrow turnpike stair is in the south-east angle, slightly corbelled out externally. A few steps lead down to the small vaulted basement chamber, which is extraordinary in having a gap in the stone flooring which opens on to a dizzy funnel-like shaft, some four feet wide, cut in the cliff-face right down to the floor of the den—for purposes uncertain, for it seems much too wide for a garderobe shute. Possibly it represents some sort of hidden exit—but there is no indication of steps having ascended the shaft.

There are vaulted chambers also on the first and second floors above, the first having a fireplace and tiny stone seats in the window embrasure. The parapet above has been carried on simple individual corbels, and there have been small open rounds at the angles.

A doorway at second-floor level gives access to the parapet-walk along the top of the curtain-wall, running parallel to the lip of the ravine. It leads to the second building, which appears to have been an L-shaped gabled structure of the late 16th or early 17th century, probably erected on the foundations of the main keep of the castle. From first-floor level a circular stair-turret is corbelled out at the south-west angle, formerly giving access to the upper floors. This building is in a bad state and the stairway has gone. At courtyard level is a vaulted chamber, and from this, following the drop in the site level, steps lead down to another vaulted cellar perhaps six feet lower. This may well have been the pit or prison of the original keep. Directly above it is still another vaulted apartment which has been converted into a strongroom for the later house. No other features of interest survive.

From as early as 1243 Lauriston, which took its name from the Chapel of St. Lawrence, belonged to the family of de Strivelyn or Stirling. They were succeeded by the Straitons, and the first of that name recorded, Alexander Stratoun de Laurenstoun, fell at the Battle of Harlaw in 1411. To this family belonged David Straiton, the early Protestant martyr who died for the Reformed faith in 1534. Sir Alexander Straiton was King's Commissioner to the General Assembly of the Kirk of Scotland meeting at Aberdeen in 1604. The Straiton lairdship came to an end in 1695 when the barony was acquired by Sir James Falconer of Phesdo.

HOUSE OF MERGIE

The modest, but substantial old mansion, known locally as the Stane Hoose o' Mergie, stands picturesquely in remote hill country off the Slug Road about six miles north-west of Stonehaven. It is a tall and plain harled building, rising from massive and rough foundations, now approximating to the T-plan, with a main block and a short stair-wing projecting centrally southwards; but this latter appears to be a later addition, and the earlier building was probably an oblong house of the 17th century, of three storeys.

[164]

There has been considerable alteration however, and even this may have been an extension of a smaller late 16th-century tower-house. The present roof-level is obviously not original. A stair-turret is corbelled out above first-floor level in the centre of the north front, with very small windows or shot-holes filled in and harled over.

The basement is not vaulted, the ceilings being very low. The kitchen had a wide arched fireplace, now filled in and modernised. The first floor is notable for the wealth of excellent pine panelling, three rooms and a lobby being so enhanced. Otherwise the interior retains no features of interest, the later stair-wing superseding the former turnpike in the corbelled turret. The building has long been used as a farmhouse.

Mergie was originally the mansion of a large estate. In 1590 the 10th Earl of Angus, of nearby Glenbervie Castle, conveyed to his youngest son, Robert Douglas various lands including The Stonehouse of Mergie, with the fortalice thereof. It is notable how this terminology has survived, when stone houses are anything but unusual. Straloch records the place on his map of the early 17th century, as Margy. In 1661 a Lt. Col. Paul Symmer is named as 'of Mergie'. He was an officer in Cromwell's army, and said to be related to the Southesk Carnegies. In 1772 Mergie was bought by Alexander Garrioch, Writer, of Edinburgh, an ardent Jacobite. Taken prisoner at Sheriffmuir, he was lodged in Stirling Castle. He had acted as Governor of Stonehaven for King James. His estate escaped confiscation by being transferred to his daughters.

Mergie was sold in 1782 to Colonel Duff of Fetteresso, with which family it remained. Robert Burns had a tiff with this laird, when poaching his water, on a visit to the district. Caught, he tossed away his rod, and fled, later to allegedly pen the lines:

> Your fish are scarce, your water's sma',
> There's my rod—and Rab's awa'!

The bard's ancestors came from this area; indeed one of them, Walter Burness who died in 1715, is said to have been tenant of The Stonehouse of Mergie.

MONBODDO HOUSE

In an estate now taken over for farming purposes, the decayed mansion of Monboddo stands about five miles north of Laurence-kirk. The ancient portion, now in a bad state structurally, consists of a simple oblong block, dating from the first half of the 17th century, two storeys and an attic in height, now somewhat altered, to which a large modern mansion has been attached. The walls are harled, the windows fairly large and regular, and corner-turrets, somewhat heavy for the dimensions of the house, crown the two northern angles. The chimneys and roof-line have been altered. A heraldic panel is centred in the west gable, displaying the arms of

Irvine or Ervine impaling those of Douglas, with the initials R.E. and I.D. and the date 1635.

The basement is not vaulted. The westernmost basement chamber was the old kitchen, containing a very large fireplace arch. Relics of panelling remain in what has been a well-proportioned Hall on the first floor, provided with two garderobes. Unfortunately all is now in a derelict condition.

Monboddo was Barclay property from the 13th century onwards, but by 1593 the laird was James Strachan or Strathauchin. Soon afterwards it passed to the Irvines and then the Burnetts, and here was born in 1714 the famous judge, James Burnett, Lord Monboddo, who anticipated the Darwinian theory, believing that men were monkeys whose tails were worn off by constant sitting. The still more famous Dr Samuel Johnson visited Monboddo in 1773 to call on the judge.

MUCHALLS CASTLE

This is one of the most interesting castles of the North-East, both for its own excellence and because it has been so little altered and added to. It stands high on a commanding site a mile inland from the sea, five miles north of Stonehaven.

Although there is older work incorporated, the house as it stands is an excellent example of early 17th-century defensive domestic architecture. Over the gateway to the courtyard a panel states: 'This work begun on the east and north be Ar. Burnet of Leyis 1619. Ended be Sir Thomas Burnet of Leyis his sonne 1627.'

The plan is the favourite L with a slight extension, the main block running east and west, the wing extending southwards at the west end, and another embryo wing projecting only slightly at the east end. Curtain-walling completes the square of a flagged courtyard. There is a semi-circular stair-tower in the main re-entrant, and there are angle-turrets at all main gables save for that of the embryo wing, which contains the main stair to first-floor level, and above is corbelled out quite elaborately to form a watch-chamber. The roof-levels have been slightly altered, and originally there was almost certainly a further attic storey. The walls are roughcast, and the range of massive chimney-stacks a feature. Open rounds enhance the curtain-walling, formerly served by a parapet and walk—although this would seem to have been as much ornamental as useful. Two sets of triple shot-holes defend the gateway. Underground vaulting and extra thick walling in

[167]

places seem to indicate the existence of an earlier fortalice on the site.

The door is in the foot of the embryo wing and admits to the stair-foot, and a vaulted passage giving access to the series of groined-vaulted basement chambers, which include the kitchen. A secondary stair rises in the circular tower, which narrows in its upper storey.

The pride of Muchalls is the handsome Great Hall on the main block first floor, a large and handsome apartment with a magnificent painted plaster ceiling, ornamented with heraldic designs of the Burnett and allied families, and medallion heads of Biblical and classic heroes. Above the enormous fireplace, with its great lintel-stone, is a fine coloured overmantel dated 1624 displaying the royal arms of Scotland. The splendour of this Hall to some extent takes away from the due appreciation of two other excellent public rooms with fine ceilings and heraldic decoration—the withdrawing-room (now the dining-room) and the laird's study, both on the first floor of the west wing. Higher there is ample bedroom accommodation. The bedroom at the west end of the main block was evidently the laird's own, for from a wall-chamber therein a listening device or 'laird's lug' communicates with the ingoing of the Hall fireplace directly below.

Before the Burnetts acquired Muchalls it was Fraser property. In 1614 the Privy Council notes that Andrew Fraser, apparent of Muchalls, accompanied by George Grant 'a noisome fighter' and others, all armed and wearing pistolets, 'dernit' themselves at the Brig o' Dee. There they attacked Alexander Bannerman of Elsick, his son and brother, wounding the brother. Fraser was fined, and his father, Laird of Muchalls had to find caution of 5,000 merks. The Council declared '. . . such ane feckles and unworthy cause as hes not been hard of in ony country subject to law and justice, to wit because the said Alex. Bannerman simply and ignorantly took the place before Fraser at the ingoing of a door'.

Whether arising out of such behaviour or otherwise, it was only five years later that the Burnetts obtained Muchalls. Alexander Burnett of Leys who began the present work was also the laird who was responsible for the completion of the well-known Crathes Castle. His son Thomas who finished the work was created a baronet of Nova Scotia in 1626.

THORNTON CASTLE

This fairly small but excellent and well-preserved example of a fortalice of the late 15th or early 16th century, stands, with a more modern mansion attached, in fairly low-lying parkland three miles west of Laurencekirk, in the Howe of the Mearns. No doubt the surroundings would be marshy at one time, to provide a defensive situation. It is an L-shaped structure of main block and stair-wing, rising four storeys to a crenellated parapet with open rounds at the angles, carried on a chequered corbel-table. The parapet-walk, drained by the usual cannon-like spouts, continues around the building, and projects as a half-round to give access past a free-standing chimney-stack on the east front. Above parapet-level the garret storey has been renewed. Lower additions of various later dates extend to north and east, the oldest of which ends in a round flanking-tower projecting to the north-east. This is decorated by a handsome heraldic panel bearing the arms of Strachan. A renewed panel on the old keep gives the date 1531, but it is probable that older work than this is incorporated. The masonry is good quality warm red coursed rubble.

Internally there has necessarily been much alteration to link up with the later additions, but many original features remain. The basement is vaulted, and now forms the vestibule for the house. The turnpike stair is wide and roomy for the period. The Hall, on the first floor, is now panelled, but there are traces of tempera painting behind it.

Originally the property belonged to a family of Thornton of that Ilk, but in 1309 an heiress carried the lands to Sir James Strathauchin or Strachan. John Strachan, knighted in 1375, obtained Thornton from his father, and the Strachans remained in

possession for thirteen generations. In 1460 John de Strathachin of Thornton was a receiver of rents for the Crown. They seem to have been good Protestants in a not over-Protestant area, for in 1590 another John Strachan of Thornton was appointed to a commission to act against Jesuits and seminary priests. In 1616 the Privy Council demanded 10,000 merks caution from Sir Alexander Strachan of Thornton, and Sir Robert Arbuthnot of that Ilk, to keep the peace between them. Two years later presumably there was still trouble, for Sir Alexander got a permit to travel abroad for three years—usually a polite form of exile. However, he was created a baronet in 1625, so he seems to have made his peace with the authorities. The 6th baronet, Admiral Sir Richard Strachan G.C.B. was a distinguished naval commander of the Napoleonic period. By his time, however, the Strachans had lost Thornton, an heiress carrying it to Robert Forbes of Newton in 1683. The last of the Strachan lairds, curiously enough became parish minister of Keith in Banffshire. He was deposed for nonconformity in 1690. A local rhyme referred to him.

> The beltit Knicht o' Thornton an' Laird o' Pittendriech,
> An' Maister James Strachan, the Minister o' Keith.

It passed after three generations to the Fullartons, then to Lord Gardenstone, and in the 19th century to the Crombies, who did much alteration. In 1893 the late Sir Thomas Thornton brought the name back to the property, by purchase. The present laird is Sir Colin Thornton-Kemsley, Baronet.

TILQUHILLIE CASTLE

On high ground two miles south-west of Banchory, Tilquhillie is a tall, plain but imposing fortalice, built in 1576, no longer occupied but in fair condition. Erected on the Z-plan, it has a semi-circular stair-tower, possibly of later date, rising in one of the main re-entrants, and a narrow stair-turret corbelled out above the first floor in the other. The walls rise to three storeys and a garret, and are unusual in that the corners are rounded up to just below eaves level, where, at all angles, they are corbelled out to the square—presumably for better roofing. The windows are mainly small and there are a number of shot-holes. The door is in the foot of the semi-circular tower and above is a worn heraldic panel. The corbelling of the slender stair-turret is unusual. The basement is vaulted.

Tilquhillie belonged to the Abbey of Arbroath, and at the Reformation presumably passed to the family of Ogstoun, for an Ogstoun heiress carried it in marriage to David Douglas, son of Douglas of Lochleven. The builder of the present house was John Douglas, possibly son of the above. He took Huntly's side against Queen Mary at the Battle of Corrichie, but through his Douglas relative, the powerful Earl of Morton, was pardoned. Later, when the Regent Morton himself was in trouble, he is said to have dwelt at Tilquhillie incognito as James the Grieve. Sir Robert Douglas of Tilquhillie was a militant royalist, and during the religious wars the castle was garrisoned by Covenanters. In 1665 a Douglas heiress carried Tilquhillie to George Crichton of Cluny.

MUCH-ALTERED STRUCTURES

A LIST, by no means exhaustive, of fortified houses, which, although dating in some part from the defensive period, and surviving, have been so altered at a later period as to leave little of the earlier work visible, and to now present a wholly different appearance.

ABERDEENSHIRE

Balquholly or Hatton Castle
Birse Castle
Blairs House
Dundarg Castle
Fetternear House
Frendraught House
Glenkindie House
Kincausie House
Knockespock House
Maryculter House
Meldrum Castle
Pitmedden House
Skene House
Warthill House

ANGUS

Auchterhouse
Bannatyne Castle
Brechin Castle
Turin House

KINCARDINESHIRE

Arbuthnott House
Brotherton Castle
Fettercairn House

ARBUTHNOTT HOUSE

The seat for untold generations of the noble family of Arbuthnott, this house at first sight, although handsome, gives little hint as to its original and fortified beginnings, seeming to be, from the front, a fairly typical Georgian mansion of the mid-18th century. But inspection at the rear presents a different picture, revealing a range of early buildings of more than one period, added as the lords of Arbuthnott required, and now difficult to put in order of construction or to describe. These enclose three sides of a courtyard. Round there, to the north, it can be seen also that the site is a defensive one, where two tributaries of the Bervie Water meet to form a sort of ravine.

One of the early parts of the range appears to have been a square tower, now reduced in height and given an ordinary gabled roof. On the east front of this are two arrow-slits at basement-level and a small

single window on the floor above, this having the outlet spout for an internal basin below it, an unusual provision at that level. More normal is another such spout projecting from the basement of a lower addition to the north. Still further to the north is a crow-stepped appendage with two small windows in the gable, that on the first floor having directly below its sill a peculiar double shot-hole of odd design. The range on the west side, not shown in sketch, has been made more modern in appearance, to match the frontage.

The first tower at Arbuthnott was built by Hugh of that name in 1420, and additions were made in 1470 and 1500, providing kitchen and domestic accommodation, these being the subsidiary buildings to the north enclosing the courtyard.

Arbuthnott was a thanage in Celtic times, gained in time by a Norman family called Oliphant, in the 11th century. In the following century, Hugh de Swinton came up from Berwickshire and married the Oliphant heiress, taking the name of Arbuthnott from the lands. From that day to this, the same family have owned the estate and resided there. Sir Robert Arbuthnott was the father of the first viscount in the early 17th century; and it was the 5th viscount who built the Georgian frontage and other additions. He was a supporter of the royal Stewart house, and portraits of the Old Pretender, his sons Prince Charles Edward and the Cardinal of York, with their mother, hang in the mansion's dining-room. The present laird is John, 16th Viscount of Arbuthnott.

AUCHLOSSAN

This substantial but much-altered former laird's-house, now a farmhouse, does not at first sight appear to belong to the fortified category and period; but closer inspection reveals that it does. It stands at the roadside about 5 miles north-east of Aboyne and 2 miles south-west of Lumphanan, in a level area which was originally under water, where was the quite large Loch of Auchlossan, which was partially drained in the late 17th century and completely so in 1859. This development has of course totally changed the defensive nature of the site.

The building, the roofline of which has been much lowered, to greatly alter the aspect, consists of an oblong block of two storeys and a garret in height, with a row of five windows at first-floor level. Unfortunately the doorway, central in he south front, is now obscured by a modern porch. It has been defended by four shot-holes. The two above are still visible and downward-pointing, and the two below now filled in. There is an empty panel-space above the porch and below the upper shot-holes. The windows are, in the main, with

chamfered surrounds; but one in the gable has a simple roll-moulding of earlier date. There is a row of seven or eight corbels projecting at eaves level at the back or north side, for purposes uncertain. The interior of the house has been modernised. It is not vaulted.

Items of its earlier aspect are to be found in subsidiary buildings, however. Two heraldic fragments are built into a barn and outhouse walling, one with the carved initial R and a scarcely identifiable charge, the other with three bougets around a boar's head. These probably came from the pediments of former dormer windows of the missing upper storey.

Andrew Rose, second son of Sir William Rose, second of Kilravock in Moray, obtained the lands of Auchlossan in 1363. The heraldic arms mentioned above are those of Rose. The eighth laird was killed at the Battle of Malplaquet in 1709, and the lands then sold to Ferguson of Pitfour, who however got the name changed to Ross. Of the earlier line came the Provost Ross of Aberdeen, whose house there is well-known, and who became first of Arnage.

BANNATYNE HOUSE

Situated on the outskirts of the pleasant village of Newtyle in Angus, this is a moderately-sized late 16th century house on the L-plan, with considerable late 18th century work added, now all lovingly restored. It is very typical in style, of three storeys, harled and whitewashed, with the main block lying east and west, a stair-tower at the north-west angle, and an angle-turret at the north-east corner, this having been provided with two shot-holes. A massive chimney-stack rises midway, above the former kitchen.

The interior has been much altered, but interesting features remain. The ground floor is not vaulted. The aforementioned kitchen has a wide-arched fireplace. There are two garderobes at first-floor level, where was the hall, each with a tiny window. Sundry former dormer-window pediments are built into the walling of the later work to the south, one of 16th century date with the initials M.T.B. for Master Thomas Bannatyne, Lord Newtyle of Session, with the arms of his wife Mariota Gilbert.

The restoration was carried out in recent years by a new owner named Bannatyne. This name is thought to be of Borders origen, like Ballantyne a corruption of Bellenden. This was the gathering-place of the Scott clan, near the head of Borthwick Water in Roxburghshire, and the word served as their slogan or war-cry - a far cry from Strathmore in Angus.

HATTON MANOR

Now a farmhouse, this former fortalice should more properly be
called the Hatton, or Hall-toun of Auchterless; its name was changed
when its lairdly family of Duff moved from here, in 1820, to rebuild
Balquhollie Castle six miles to the north-east, and took the style of
Hatton Castle with them. This is the Duff line, which rose to the
earldom of MacDuff and dukedom of Fife, although from
comparatively humble beginnings.

Hatton Manor, situated half-a-mile west of the Kirkton of
Auchterless and some six miles south of Turriff, is a fairly plain
building of the 16th and later 17th centuries, L-planned, with a
circular stair-tower projecting on the north front. The east end has
been added to and altered. The roof has been lowered, which detracts
from the appearance and leaves the gables without their crowsteps.
There is a 16th century roll-moulding at the doorway on the south
front, but most of the window-surrounds have chamfered edges of
later date. Two circular and one square shot-holes defend the north
front; and the only other feature of note surviving is the skewputt on

the west gable, inscribed with the initials W.M. and the figures 92. This last probably refers to the date 1692 when the alterations would be made, the initials being for the Mowat family, here before the Duffs purchased the property. The Mowats main seat was at the aforementioned Balquhollie Castle, to which the Duffs removed; they were an important Aberdeen family in the old days, their name being originally the Norman Montealto, which of course just means high land. Interestingly, not far away is a site called Moat Head, the place for formerly holding baronial courts; no doubt the name is merely a corruption of Mowat. This Hatton would be only a secondary seat.

AUTHOR'S NOTE

Some small number of the ruinous buildings described herein have been, or are being, restored to make homes again — to the great satisfaction of the writer.

INDEX

INDEX TO ADDENDA